ACCOUNTING AND FINANCIAL FUNDAMENTALS FOR NONFINANCIAL EXECUTIVES

ACCOUNTING AND FINANCIAL FUNDAMENTALS FOR NONFINANCIAL EXECUTIVES

2nd Edition

Robert Rachlin & Allen Sweeny

amacom

American Management Association

New York • Atlanta • Boston • Chicago • Kansas City • San Francisco • Washington, D. C.
Brussels • Mexico City • Tokyo • Toronto

Library of Congress Cataloging-in-Publication Data

Rachlin, Robert, 1937–
      Accounting and financial fundamentals for nonfinancial executives
 / Robert Rachlin & Allen Sweeny.—2nd ed.
      p.   cm.
      Rev. ed. of: Accounting fundamentals for nonfinancial executives /
 Allen Sweeny. 1972.
      Includes index.
      ISBN 0-8144-7928-6 ISBN 978-0-8144-7928-5
      1. Accounting.   I. Sweeny, Allen.   II. Sweeny, Allen.
 Accounting fundamentals for nonfinancial executives.
 HF5635.R114   1996
 657'024'658—dc20   95-45925
                                                                      CIP

*Portions of this book are revised versions of chapters originally pub-
lished as* Accounting Fundamentals for Nonfinancial Executives
by Allen Sweeny.

Printing number

10   9   8   7   6   5   4

To
Brian, Matthew, and Jeremy
and
to
Donna

Contents

Preface

The field of basic accounting and finance frankly offers little that is new or exciting in terms of content.

Literally hundreds of books have been written on these two subjects, and this revised edition, like the original, has been written with definite if more modest and (as its title suggests) "fundamental" purposes:

1. To simplify basic accounting and also many financial concepts
2. To present these ideas as briefly and clearly as possible

As was the case with the original edition, we have assumed that the reader is a nonfinancial executive with virtually no prior knowledge of accounting and finance and—equally important—that he or she has neither the time nor the inclination to wade through a thousand-page textbook to correct the situation.

The sixteen concise chapters that follow (which, in this revised edition, have been expanded to cover the fundamentals of cost, investment, ROI, cash flow, and financial analysis) will, we hope, provide a readable alternative remedy that requires little time or effort.

ACCOUNTING AND FINANCIAL FUNDAMENTALS FOR NONFINANCIAL EXECUTIVES

1

The Dual Aspect Principle

Accounting is frequently called the language of business. Undoubtedly many people feel that this particular description lends undue glamour to the often confusing and mysterious black art of bookkeeping. Still, the fact remains that accounting and finance are the primary tools for reducing business problems and opportunities to a common denominator, setting goals, measuring results, and making decisions.

An understanding of the basic concepts of accounting and finance is critical to the successful performance of all executives and businesspersons, whether they like it or not. This book presents those concepts in as simple and straightforward a manner as possible. The following pages will certainly not train any accountants. We do hope, however, that they will help the busy nonfinancial executive to become knowledgeable about (1) fundamental accounting and financial concepts and practices and (2) the uses, as well as the limitations, of those practices in the managerial process.

To do this, we shall place more emphasis on concepts and essentials and less on explanations of debits, credits, and ledgers, since our purpose is to explain how to use, rather than how to create, financial data. More important, we shall concentrate on the inherently commonsensical aspects of the accounting and financial function. In adopting this approach, there is no intent to downgrade the exacting and critical role of the professional accountant. Nor should the reader assume that the accounting and financial transactions of large and complex business organizations are always simple. The point, rather, is that the basic concepts that underlie the accounting function are the keys to understanding it and are often amazingly simple.

To explore these propositions more specifically, let's begin with the two concepts that are at the heart of all accounting theory and practice: the **dual aspect principle,** discussed in this chapter, and the **accrual concept,** discussed in Chapter 2.

We can illustrate the dual aspect principle with a hypothetical but common personal situation, the purchase of a home. This activity involves the screening and then the selection of the house to be bought. Finally, the necessary financing must be arranged. Assume that the house can be purchased for $130,000 and that to make this purchase, you wish to borrow $100,000, which is to be financed through a conventional 30-year mortgage loan.

The rub, of course, is that you must convince some friendly banker of your credit worthiness. To evaluate your credit standing, he or she will want to know whether you can make the necessary down payment on the house and then repay the mortgage loan with interest over the next 30 years. In other words, what are you worth? The process used to determine this information is not especially complex.

First, the banker will want to know what things of value you own and how much money you owe and to whom. Assume that your response to these questions looks like this:

Things of Value		Amount Owed	
Cash		Personal bank loan	$20,000
Checking account	$ 5,000		
Savings	15,500		
Stock at current			
market value	29,500		
Total	$50,000		

For the sake of brevity, assume that your personal financial situation meets with approval and that you (along with your friendly banker) now become happy homeowners. As a result of this transaction, your financial situation now looks like this:

Things of Value		Amount Owed	
Cash			
Checking account	$ 5,000		
Stock	15,000	Personal bank loan	$ 20,000
House	130,000	30-year mortgage loan	100,000
Total	$150,000	Total	$120,000

Through this simple and familiar process, you have not only become homeowners but have also made use of some key accounting concepts. For example, one of the basic facts in which your banker was interested was what things of value you owned. The same question could be phrased as, What are your assets? **Assets** is the word accountants use to describe things of value. Others, of course, also use this term, but the accountant uses it to describe something of value measurable in monetary terms. This approach was used in your bank application. Even if you are blessed with excellent health, good looks, and a dynamic personality, these assets—no matter how valuable—are not readily measurable in monetary terms and therefore cannot be listed as assets in your loan application.

Second, you were asked to list what you owed and to whom. In general as well as in accounting terminology, such obligations are referred to as **liabilities** and represent a legal commitment. To be legally obligated is, in fact, to be liable. Another way to think of liabilities is as a claim on your assets. The person to whom you are liable has a claim on your assets up to the amount of credit extended to you. Another word for such a claim is **equity**. Special courts, called courts of equity, specialize in the just and impartial settlement of contending claims. In our particular illustration, your creditor (the bank) extended to you a personal loan of $20,000, and you were liable for a claim on assets in this amount. In this case and all others, the claim of the creditor on these assets is a liability.

If this liability is $20,000, there are obviously still $30,000 of assets to be claimed, and the next logical question is: Who has a claim on these? If no other creditors have a claim on these assets, obviously you, the owner, have a claim on them, and they are called **owner's equity**. Thus, there can be two types of equities (claims against your assets)—liabilities, or claims of lenders or creditors, and owner's equity, or claims of the owners.

In terms of assets, liabilities, and equities, the financial information on the loan application before and after purchase would appear as follows:

BEFORE PURCHASE

Assets		*Equities*	
Cash			
Checking account	$ 5,000	Liabilities	
Savings	15,500	Personal loan	$ 20,000
Stock at current			
market value	29,500	Owner's equity	30,000
Total assets	$50,000	Total assets	$ 50,000

AFTER PURCHASE

Assets		*Equities*	
Cash		Liabilities	
Checking account	$ 5,000	Personal loan	$ 20,000
Stock	15,000	Mortgage loan	100,000
House	130,000	Owner's equity	30,000
Total assets	$150,000	Total equities	$150,000

We can see by comparing these tables that although you now own a home, your personal, or owner's, equity remains unchanged after the purchase. The reason is that although your assets increased, a corresponding increase has occurred in the creditor's claim on those assets.

Consider an additional point. We have said that two groups can have claims on assets—creditors and owners. Creditors are legally entitled to the first claim, and the balance that remains is the owner's equity. Thus, neither the creditors, nor the owners, nor the two groups together can have total claims on the assets that are in excess of the *total* assets. A corollary of this axiom states that *assets must always equal equities,* or (since equities may take the form of liabilities and also owner's equity), *assets must also always equal liabilities plus owner's equity.*

The fact that assets equal equities is the basic principle of all accounting theory and practice. It is often referred to as the basic accounting equation and is sometimes called the **dual aspect principle.** Accounting systems are based on the inherent logic of this principle, and all business transactions are recorded in terms of their dual effect on assets and equities.

Our illustration involved a single business transaction—the purchase of a home. The two aspects of this transaction were:

1. To show an increase in assets in the amount of $100,000, with an equal increase in equities (creditor's equities) in the same amount. (All accounting systems based on the dual aspect principle are of necessity described as **double-entry bookkeeping systems.**)
2. To point out in general terms three basic concepts: assets as things of measurable monetary value; liabilities as creditor's claims against assets; and owner's equities as the claims of owners on assets.

We can take these same concepts and, using exactly the same approach, see how they apply in a highly simplified business situation involving Gerry Manero's Furniture Mart.

After working for many years as head salesman for a local furniture manufacturer, Gerry has decided to open his own furniture store. To do this, he plans to use his personal cash savings in the amount of $15,000. If Gerry goes into business on July 27, 19X5, his accountant, using the foregoing concepts, will describe the balance of Gerry's assets and equities as follows:

GERRY MANERO'S FURNITURE MART
Balance of Assets and Equities
July 27, 19X5

Assets		Equities	
Cash	$15,000	Owner's equity	$15,000

If, on July 30, Gerry purchases an old, used delivery truck, the accountant will show this revised situation as follows:

GERRY MANERO'S FURNITURE MART
Balance of Assets and Equities
July 30, 19X5

Assets		Equities	
Cash	$10,000	Owner's equity	$15,000
Delivery truck	5,000		
Total assets	$15,000		

Similarly, a decision executed a week later to obtain a $5,000 loan will prompt the accountant to reflect another change in Gerry's financial situation:

GERRY MANERO'S FURNITURE MART
Balance of Assets and Equities
August 6, 19X5

Assets		Equities	
		Liabilities	
Cash	$15,000	Bank loan	$ 5,000
Truck	5,000	Owner's equity	15,000
Total assets	$20,000	Total equities	$20,000

We'll return to Gerry's entrepreneurial endeavor, but for the moment let's examine what the accountant has done to this point. By applying the same concepts we used in our home purchase illustration, he has prepared a financial evaluation of Gerry's new business on July 27, July 30, and August 6. This evaluation, like the loan application in our first illustration, represents the balance of the assets and equities of the business as it stood on these dates.

In accounting, such a statement is called a **balance sheet**. It is one of two basic accounting documents used to report on the financial condition of a company. Its name is well chosen, since it (1) always shows a balance of assets and equities and (2) must always balance assets and equities, as we've already seen from the dual aspect concept.

Under normal business circumstances, the balance of assets and equities being reported in a balance sheet is constantly changing. For example, each of the three balance sheets shown for the furniture mart is different from the others as a result of the business Gerry Manero transacts on each of those days. To put it another way, the asset cash in almost any company can change several times during one day or even within one hour.

Thus, a balance sheet can reflect the status of assets and equities only at a given moment. For this reason, the balance sheet is always dated, and that date is critical to a clear understanding of the financial information being presented.

Most companies prepare a formal balance sheet at least once annually, usually as of the end of the year. Clearly, the elementary nature of Gerry Manero's financial affairs simplifies the preparation of a balance sheet in his business; however, the same basic concepts are used regardless of the size or complexity of the business.

For example, Exhibit 1-1 shows the balance sheet of another GM—not Gerry Manero but General Motors, one of the world's largest industrial organizations.

As you look at the GM balance sheet, note the prominence of its date, which indicates the exact day of the status report on the company's assets and equities. Next, note that the left side of the statement lists the assets owned by the corporation. (Some or all of the various technical classifications of assets, liabilities, and equities shown on the GM balance sheet may be unfamiliar to you. At this point, we can ignore that fact, for we are looking at balance sheets in very broad conceptual terms and will present a more detailed discussion of their makeup in Chapter 3.)

The right side of the statement lists the claims on the company's assets. As in the two simpler cases already presented, these are the claims of the creditors, or the liabilities. (There are also a series of claims called **reserves,** which in this instance, as in many others, represent claims on assets that can be made by employees as a result of benefit payments that the company is legally commit-

Exhibit 1-1. General Motors Corporation consolidated balance sheet, December 31, 1993.

(Dollars in millions, except per share amounts)	December 31,	
Assets	**1993**	**1992**
Cash and cash equivalents	**$ 13,790.5**	$ 11,078.6
Other marketable securities	**4,172.2**	4,029.1
Total cash and marketable securities (Note 10)	**17,962.7**	15,107.7
Finance receivables—net (Note 11)	**53,874.7**	66,314.1
Accounts and notes receivable (less allowances)	**6,389.2**	6,476.7
Inventories (less allowances) (Note 1)	**8,615.1**	9,343.6
Contracts in process (less advances and progress payments of $2,739.2 and $4,026.4) (Note 1)	**2,376.8**	2,456.4
Net equipment on operating leases (less accumulated depreciation of $4,579.6 and $3,987.6)	**13,095.3**	11,286.9
Deferred income taxes (Note 8)	**20,798.1**	18,583.3
Other assets (less allowances)	**17,757.3**	15,762.1
Property (Note 1)		
Real estate, plants, and equipment—at cost (Note 13)	**67,966.4**	68,833.6
Less accumulated depreciation (Note 13)	**41,725.5**	41,462.5
Net real estate, plants, and equipment	**26,240.9**	27,371.1
Special tools—at cost (less amortization)	**7,983.9**	7,979.1
Total property	**34,224.8**	35,350.2
Intangible assets—at cost (less amortization) (Notes 1 and 4)	**13,106.9**	9,515.0
Total assets	**$188,200.9**	$190,196.0

Exhibit 1-1. *(continued)*

	December 31,	
(Dollars in millions, except per share amounts)	**1993**	**1992**
Liabilities and stockholders' equity		
Liabilities		
Accounts payable (principally trade)	**$ 10,276.5**	$ 9,678.4
Notes and loans payable (Note 14)	**70,441.2**	82,592.3
United States, foreign, and other income taxes—deferred and payable (Note 8)	**2,409.3**	3,140.1
Postretirement benefits other than pensions (Note 5)	**37,920.0**	35,550.7
Pensions (Note 4)	**22,631.6**	13,756.2
Other liabilities and deferred credits (Note 15)	**38,474.8**	38,487.7
Total Liabilities	**182,153.4**	183,205.4
Stocks Subject to Repurchase (Note 16)	**450.0**	765.0
Stockholders' Equity (Notes 3 and 16)		
Preferred stocks	**—**	234.4
Preference stocks	**4.2**	4.5
Common stocks		
$1-2/3 par value (issued, 720,105,471 and 706,831,567 shares)	**1,200.2**	1,178.1
Class E (issued, 263,089,320 and 242,168,653 shares)	**26.3**	24.2
Class H (issued, 75,705,433 and 70,240,927 shares)	**7.6**	7.0
Capital surplus (principally additional paid-in capital)	**12,003.4**	10,971.2
Accumulated deficit	(**2,002.9**)	(3,354.2)
Subtotal	**11,238.8**	9,065.2
Minimum pension liability adjustment (Note 4)	(**5,311.2**)	(2,925.3)
Accumulated foreign currency translation adjustments and net unrealized gains (losses) on marketable equity securities	(**330.1**)	85.7
Total stockholders' equity	**5,597.5**	6,225.6
Total liabilities and stockholders' equity	**$188,200.9**	$190,196.0

Certain amounts for 1992 have been reclassified to conform with 1993 classifications.
Reference should be made to the Notes to Financial Statements.

ted to pay.) The final section on the right is entitled **stockholders' equity.** GM is a corporation, so this is another way of representing the owner's equity.

The size and complexity of the assets, liabilities, and equities of a company may vary, but the basic concepts involved in preparing a balance sheet for them remain unchanged—and simple. These concepts are as applicable to the most modest proprietorships and/or partnerships, as well as to the largest corporations. They also apply to the accounting processes of all forms of business endeavor, whether a merchandising or manufacturing entity or the more common organization that combines both these activities. They also apply to the growing number of businesses whose product is a service, such as the Olsten Corporation, one of the nation's leading providers of human resource and health care services, whose 1994 balance sheet is shown in Exhibit 1-2.

Exhibit 1-2. The Olsten Corporation balance sheet, January 2, 1994.

(Dollars in thousands, except share amounts)	**January 2, 1994**	January 3, 1993
ASSETS		
Current assets		
Cash	**$ 24,709**	$ 33,297
Receivables, less allowance for doubtful accounts of $15,532 and $13,206, respectively	**325,122**	304,732
Refundable and deferred taxes (Note 7)	**43,375**	17,224
Prepaid expenses and other current assets	**13,432**	20,101
Total current assets	**406,638**	375,354
Fixed assets, net (Note 3)	**60,185**	47,614
Intangibles, principally goodwill, net of accumulated amortization of $52,059 and $46,569, respectively	**204,670**	235,778
Other assets	**18,601**	3,245
	$690,094	$661,991

Exhibit 1-2. (continued)

(Dollars in thousands, except share amounts)	January 2, 1994	January 3, 1993
LIABILITIES AND SHAREHOLDERS' EQUITY		
Current liabilities		
Accrued expenses (Note 2)	**$ 74,251**	$ 42,873
Insurance costs	**45,730**	25,359
Payroll and related taxes	**31,143**	49,747
Accounts payable	**12,597**	13,742
Current portion of long-term debt	**1,886**	12,749
Total current liabilities	**165,607**	144,470
Long-term debt (Note 4)	**176,057**	150,419
Other liabilities	**44,110**	48,380
Commitments (Note 10)	**—**	—
Shareholders' equity (Notes 2, 5, and 6)		
Common stocks $.10 par value; authorized 110,000,000 shares; issued 29,976,240 shares and 17,243,517 shares, respectively	**2,998**	1,724
Class B common stock $.10 par value; authorized 50,000,000 shares; issued 10,482,514 shares and 21,364,056 shares, respectively	**1,048**	2,136
Additional paid-in capital	**211,331**	188,772
Retained earnings	**90,280**	124,884
Cumulative translation adjustment	**(1,337)**	1,206
Total shareholders' equity	**304,320**	318,722
	$690,094	$661,991

In all cases, accounting data have both internal and external users. Internal users are managers and other decision makers who need to know the answers to questions such as how much cash is available to meet debts and operating needs; what products/services cost and their relative profitability; and where and how much resources to allocate.

There are two types of external users—those with direct interest who are directly affected by accounting results, such as creditors and investors, and those who are indirectly interested in how a company has performed, such as governmental agencies (i.e., the Internal Revenue Service and the Securities and Exchange Commission) and outside interests such as customers, stock market analysts, competitors, and potential investors.

2

The Accrual Concept

In Chapter 1 we saw that the dual aspect principle is the conceptual touchstone of all accounting theory but that it also has particular application to the preparation of one of the fundamental accounting statements, the balance sheet. In this chapter we look at a second basic concept—the accrual principle—and examine its relationship to another basic accounting document, the **income statement.**

The accrual concept is a rather nettlesome notion, since most of us tend to conduct our personal financial affairs on a cash rather than an accrual basis. We tend to view our personal financial situation in light of how much cash or how many liquid assets we have on hand. Likewise, we think of our annual net income on a gross basis, or at best after taxes; we never, however, deduct the real depreciation on our automobile or the wear and tear associated with the use of household and personal effects. Depreciation will be discussed in Chapter 6; for now, let's return to Gerry Manero and continue to record the development of his new furniture mart. The initial three transactions described in Chapter 1 result in simplified balance sheets, as shown below.

Event: July 27. Gerry Manero decides to enter the furniture business and invests $15,000 of his personal savings.

GERRY MANERO'S FURNITURE MART
Balance Sheet
July 27, 19X5

Assets		Equity	
Cash	$15,000	Owner's equity	$15,000

Event: July 30. Gerry Manero purchases an old, used delivery truck for his business.

GERRY MANERO'S FURNITURE MART
Balance Sheet
July 30, 19X5

Assets		Equity	
Cash	$10,000	Owner's equity	$15,000
Delivery truck	5,000		
Total assets	$15,000		

Event: August 6. Gerry Manero obtains a $5,000 bank loan for his new business.

GERRY MANERO'S FURNITURE MART
Balance Sheet
August 6, 19X5

Assets		Equities	
		Liabilities	
Cash	$15,000	Bank loan	$ 5,000
Delivery Truck	5,000	Owner's equity	15,000
Total assets	$20,000	Total equities	$20,000

Let's continue this process with comments on the transactions that follow.

Event: September 6. Gerry Manero purchases merchandise for $6,000 to be resold, paying cash. (Merchandise that is purchased or manufactured by a business and held for eventual sale is called **inventory**.)

GERRY MANERO'S FURNITURE MART
Balance Sheet
September 6, 19X5

Assets		Equities	
Cash	$ 9,000	Liabilities	
Merchandise inventory	6,000	Bank loan	$ 5,000
Delivery truck	5,000	Owner's equity	15,000
Total assets	$20,000	Total equities	$20,000

Event: September 8. Gerry Manero sells for $600 in cash merchandise that cost $500.

Since this particular transaction presents a slightly new wrinkle involving Gerry's first sale (the exchange of goods for a price), let's follow its effect on the balance sheet step by step.

The effect on assets is relatively clear-cut. The cash asset increases from $9,000 to $9,600 as a result of cash received from the sale. On the other hand, inventory decreases by the amount of $500 (the cost of the merchandise sold). The other asset on the balance sheet, the truck, remains unchanged at $5,000. So, in total, Gerry Manero's assets now amount to $20,100:

Assets	
Cash	$ 9,600
Inventory	5,500
Truck	5,000
Total assets	$20,100

On the equity side of the balance sheet, the liability of a $5,000 loan, payable to the bank, remains unchanged. At first glance, owner's equity of $15,000 would also appear to remain the same. If this were the case, however, the total equities of $20,000 would be less than the assets of $20,100. We know this can't be correct, since the dual aspect concept states that assets must always equal equities. For the basic accounting equation to match, total equities must also equal $20,100. We can see why they should. The bank's claim of $5,000 on the assets has not changed. There are $15,100 of assets to be claimed, and these can now be claimed only by the owner. Gerry Manero's equity—that is, his owner's equity—has increased $100. The reason, of course, is that the $500 asset of merchandise was exchanged for another asset, cash of $600. All these changes result in a September 8 balance sheet that looks like this:

GERRY MANERO'S FURNITURE MART
Balance Sheet
September 8, 19X5

Assets		Equities	
Cash	$ 9,600	Liabilities	
Merchandise inventory	5,500	Bank loan	$ 5,000
Delivery truck	5,000	Owner's equity	15,100
Total assets	$20,100	Total equities	$20,100

Event: September 10. Gerry Manero purchases $2,000 of merchandise and agrees to pay for it within 60 days. In this transaction, Gerry charges his purchase as you might charge a personal purchase at a department store. Such a charge represents a liability, since you do not own the merchandise. This particular type of liability is called an **account payable** and appears on this balance sheet:

GERRY MANERO'S FURNITURE MART
Balance Sheet
September 10, 19X5

Assets		Equities	
		Liabilities	
Cash	$ 9,600	Accounts payable	$ 2,000
Merchandise inventory	7,500	Bank loan	5,000
Delivery truck	5,000	Owner's equity	15,100
Total assets	$22,100	Total equities	$22,100

Event: September 12. Gerry Manero sells for $800 merchandise that cost $600. The customer agrees to pay the total amount in 30 days.

The effect of this transaction is the same as the effect of the transaction that took place on September 8. The only difference is that instead of receiving cash outright, the furniture mart has received the promise of payment within 30 days. Although not cash, this promise represents an asset that is called an **account receivable.** It appears in this balance sheet:

GERRY MANERO'S FURNITURE MART
Balance Sheet
September 12, 19X5

Assets		Equities	
Cash	$ 9,600	Liabilities	
Accounts receivable	800	Accounts payable	$ 2,000
Merchandise inventory	6,900	Bank loan	5,000
Delivery truck	5,000	Owner's equity	15,300
Total assets	$22,300	Total equities	$22,300

Event: September 15. Gerry Manero sells for $1,000 merchandise that cost $700. The customer pays cash.

Here again, this transaction affects owner's equity in the same manner as the sales on September 8 and 12.

GERRY MANERO'S FURNITURE MART
Balance Sheet
September 15, 19X5

Assets		Equities	
Cash	$10,600	Liabilities	
Accounts receivable	800	Accounts payable	$ 2,000
Merchandise inventory	6,200	Bank loan	5,000
Delivery truck	5,000	Owner's equity	15,600
Total assets	$22,600	Total equities	$22,600

Let's stop now to compare the first and the last balance sheets for the furniture mart.

GERRY MANERO'S FURNITURE MART
Comparative Balance Sheet

Assets	July 27	Sept. 15	Equities	July 27	Sept. 15
			Liabilities		
Cash	$15,000	$10,600	Accounts payable		$ 2,000
Accounts			Loan payable		5,000
receivable		800	Subtotal		$ 7,000
Inventory		6,200	Owner's equity	$15,000	15,600
Delivery truck		5,000			
Total assets	$15,000	$22,600	Total equities	$15,000	$22,600

We note, first, that the furniture mart has increased its assets and equities by $7,600. Second, and more important, owner's equity, that is, Gerry Manero's equity, has increased $600. This occurred because the assets of merchandise were exchanged for another asset—cash—at a higher value. In accounting terms, such an increase in owner's equity is called **income** or **profit**. It is important to remember that when the accountant refers to income, he or she is concerned exclusively with increases in owner's equity. Thus, on August 6, the furniture mart's total assets increased $5,000, but because liabilities simultaneously increased in the same amount, there was no change in owner's equity and therefore no income.

Actually, only three transactions of the furniture mart had an effect on owner's equity. These were the sales of merchandise on September 8, 12, and 15. On the 8th and the 15th, owner's equity increased at the same time cash increased because the customer paid money for the merchandise. On September 12, however, equity increased while cash remained unchanged because the customer bought the merchandise on credit. Increases in owner's equity, therefore, do not depend on increases or decreases in cash. Rather, owner's equity changes, as in both these cases, because the monies obtained are greater than the costs of the goods sold.

These sales increased the owner's equity. In accounting, an increase in owner's equity is called **revenue**. The process of turning the goods over to the customer, however, brought about a decrease in the owner's equity in the amount that was paid for the goods sold. This decrease in owner's equity is called an **expense**. The difference between the revenue (an increase in owner's equity) and the expense (the decrease in owner's equity) is **net income**.

The distinctive aspect of the three business transactions that affected owner's equity was not whether cash was increased or decreased but whether revenues were greater than expenses. The concept that net income is measured by increases or decreases in owner's equity rather than by increases or decreases in cash is called the **accrual concept.**

The dual aspect concept has particular relevance to the accounting document of the balance sheet. The accrual concept is basic to the second fundamental accounting document, the **income statement.**

We can summarize our comments on the conceptual basis for an income statement as follows:

1. In accounting, increases in owner's equity that arise from the sale and exchange of a good or service are called net income.

2. When a business provides a good or service, the monies it receives increase owner's equity and are called revenues.
3. The costs that business incurs to provide the good or service decrease the owner's equity and are called expenses.
4. Under the accrual concept, net income is measured by the difference between revenues and expenses, *not* by increases or decreases in cash.

An income statement summarizes the revenues and expenses of a business over a given period of time and reflects the difference between the two as net income if revenues are greater than expenses. If expenses are greater than revenues, there has not been a net income to the owners, and the result is shown as a **net loss.**

A term that is often used interchangeably with net income is profit. Thus, an income statement is also referred to as a statement of profit and/or loss (often abbreviated P/L statement). The choice is only one of terminology, since the purpose and the concept of the statement are the same under either label.

An income statement for Gerry Manero's Furniture Mart for the period between July 27 and September 15 would appear as follows:

GERRY MANERO'S FURNITURE MART
Income Statement
Period Ending September 15, 19X5

Revenues	$2,400
Less cost of goods sold	1,800
Net income	$ 600

The source of these figures is as follows:

Revenues are increases to owner's equity through sales of merchandise:

September 8	$ 600
September 12	800
September 15	1,000
Total revenues as per income statement	$2,400

Expenses represent decreases to owner's equity for the costs associated with providing these goods:

September 8	$ 500
September 12	600
September 15	700
Total expenses as per income statement	$1,800

Revenues minus expenses equal net income, or $600, which is the net income to owner's equity for the period July 27 through September 15.

Our income statement shows the same net increase to owner's equity as the comparison of the balance sheets of the furniture mart for July 27 and September 15. This is as expected, since net income represents the increase in owner's equity that takes place through the conduct of a company's business.

In theory, the total net income of a business over its entire life is simply the amount the owners get out of it compared to what they originally put in. It is possible to measure the net income of business this way. The owner's equity could be calculated after 10 years of business activity and compared with the owner's original equity. If there has been an increase, as there should have been, this would be the net income of the business for the total 10-year period. Although an accountant could measure the net income of a business this way, it is not practical for two reasons:

1. Neither management nor the owners of a business can wait until the 10-year period is over to see how the business has fared.

2. Management and owners want to know more specifically when the increase in owner's equity occurred—evenly over the life of the business, in the beginning, or at the end?

For these reasons, determinations of net income are made at frequent intervals over the life of the business in an income statement. In most countries it is customary (and in some, mandatory) for businesses to prepare an income statement at least once a year. Almost all publicly held corporations in the United States prepare income statements for each calendar quarter and issue them to the public and to their shareholders. For its own internal use, management may have income statements prepared on a monthly basis.

Our accounting efforts on behalf of Gerry Manero obviously remain simple; although we have touched on only the fundamentals of an income statement, we have a foundation to build on in subsequent chapters. First, however, a few more basics.

3

Other Basic Concepts

The essayist and poet Ralph Waldo Emerson once said, "The value of a principle is the number of things it will explain." The truth of this statement is nowhere more apparent than in the field of accounting. In Chapters 1 and 2 we looked at two key principles that explain much of accounting theory and practice. In this chapter, we discuss five significant but less important principles that also explain the work of the accountant.

The Money Measurement Principle

This **money measurement principle** simply says that accounting measures business transactions only in terms of money. This idea seems too obvious to require discussion. There are, however, an infinite number of ways to account for things—in terms of grades, in terms of qualitative appraisals such as good, satisfactory, excellent, and so on. Accounting, however, measures things *only* in terms of money.

This approach has several advantages. First, it provides a simple measuring device, which allows a variety of different facts to be expressed in a common denominator. For example, a large steel plant can be compared to a research laboratory when both are expressed in monetary terms. Second, when things are expressed in monetary terms, they can be dealt with mathematically. Thus, different types of buildings, equipment, and machinery cannot only be cast in terms of a common denominator but also be added, subtracted, and otherwise manipulated to express various aspects of the business.

Although the money measurement principle brings obvious and necessary advantages to the accounting process, however, it simultaneously imposes severe limitations, since the most valuable assets of a business are often intangible. Perhaps the best example of this fact is the great but intangible value of the skills of employees and management in a business. No one has yet devised a way to quantify these skills in terms of money, and therefore they cannot be shown to an accounting reader as part of the value of the business. Other important assets that cannot be accounted for in monetary terms include technological know-how, reputation, and brand awareness.

As the old saying goes, "money isn't everything." Accounting reports include only those events that can be reduced to a monetary basis and thus may ignore some of the most important facets of a business. Recognition of this fact is the beginning of the wise and intelligent use of accounting information.

The Business Entity Principle

The **business entity principle** is another rather simple notion. It means that accounting keeps records for business entities, rather than for individuals.

Suppose, for example, that Gerry Manero withdraws $150 from his furniture mart's checking account. Since he is the sole owner of this business, he is now $150 richer, the business has $150 less, and there has been no overall change in Gerry's total cash position. The accountant, however, would record only the effect of this transaction on the business. In other words, the accountant would show that the business now has $150 less and would ignore the effect of this transaction on Gerry. Transactions, therefore, can affect the owner of a business in one way and the business itself in another way.

The business entity principle obviously has limited relevance for the accounting function of the established major corporation. Many a public accountant has burned the midnight oil, however, in an effort to apply this concept to the combined personal and business records of the individual proprietor.

The Going Concern Principle

Most businesses begin with the basic idea that they will be operated in a logical, rational manner that will lead to success over an extended period of time. This same basic assumption is made by the accountant and is called the **going concern principle**. It facilitates the accountant's difficult job of assessing values. To see why this is so, we must discuss the cost concept.

The Cost Concept

Cost, as we all know, doesn't necessarily equal value. The fact is that in today's world, stock market investors buy and trade millions of shares of stocks of companies for prices far in excess of their "book" or cost value. The cost concept has its problems and limitations, but no one in the accounting profession has yet been able to come up with an acceptable alternative that provides the same practicality and objectivity.

As we saw in Chapter 1, the listing of assets is a key step in preparing a balance sheet. Certainly, it is one of the most basic functions of the accountant. The foundation on which the value of these assets is to be established is obviously a key question. The answer is not as clear-cut as it might appear.

To illustrate, let's again use an example of home ownership. Suppose one morning a prospective buyer looks at your home and asks you what you consider to be its value. Later on in the day, a tax assessor comes to look at your home and asks the same question. Most of us would give one answer to the prospective buyer and another to the tax assessor, whether or not we are honest enough to admit it. The point is that the assessment of value can be a highly subjective process. Herein lies the dilemma. The accountant must bring objectivity to the valuation of a business. For this reason the problem of how to value the assets of a business is an important as well as a nettlesome question. There are three possibilities.

1. *Value the assets at their market value.* Simple enough—just state the worth of the property today. But this isn't always as easy as it sounds. The value of something can be highly dependent upon the prospective purchaser's particular needs; for this reason, it's possible to get three, four, or five differing evaluations of the worth of any particular property. The economists call this the theory of **utility**. However, an accountant who uses this concept will again run directly into the problem of subjectivity.

2. *Value the assets on the basis of the amount of money that would be required to replace them.* This replacement value does away with a value range that depends on the prospective buyer's needs. The cost of replacing something, however, often depends on how it is replaced. For example, it's standard practice in most businesses to obtain at least three or four bids before major construction is undertaken. The reason, of course, is that the cost can vary depending on who does the work, what material they use, how efficiently they go about the construction, and other factors. The use of a replacement approach almost always provides a range rather than a single common value to place on the asset.

3. *Determine the value of any particular asset on the basis of its original cost.* The advantage of this particular approach, of course, is that it's easy to determine and subsequently document exactly what you paid for something. For example, how would you get a variety of opinions about the value of your attaché case? Some opinions may be based on its so-called market value, some possibly on its replacement value. The one cost that you and others could agree on, however, would be the cost you originally incurred to buy it. To establish this cost, you need only to produce the original invoice. This does not necessarily suggest that everyone would agree that you had made a good buy. The fact remains that you can, on the basis of the original cost, objectively establish the value of the case. This is the so-called **cost concept.**

The objective approach is extremely important to the accountant, and its practical advantages are obvious. The cost concept gives the accountant a simple, workable method by which to record asset values on a balance sheet. Executives and business-people who understand this concept always know immediately the basis for the asset values that appear in any balance sheet, since under the cost concept they are always recorded at original cost.

The primary appeal of the cost concept is its expediency and objectivity. As we noted earlier, however, the going concern concept is also relevant to the question of determining asset values. Under that principle, the accountant assumes that there will be little likelihood of the need to determine asset values in liquidation. Because it is assumed that the assets will be used in the normal conduct of the business rather than sold or disposed of, the question of the value of the assets does not become as critical as it might otherwise. In this way the going concern principle facilitates the accounting problem of determining the values of assets.

The Realization Principle

A routine business transaction often involves more steps than meet the eye. Let's take, for example, a fictitious company—EZI Manufacturing Company—and its sale of widgets. In December, the widgets were manufactured at the factory. In January, the widgets were shipped to the customer, who paid EZI part of the bill for the widgets in February and the rest in March. In total, this rather simple business transaction has spanned a period of four months.

The question for the accountant is: When did the business actually obtain its sales revenue? The more formal statement of the problem is: When was the business's revenue "realized"? To answer this question, the accountant uses the realization principle.

This principle, like so many of the others, is simple. It says that revenue is realized at the time goods or services are furnished.

Applying the principle to the EZI transaction, we would say that the revenue was realized for the company in January, when the merchandise was delivered. Under the realization principle, a business cannot record or account for sales revenue until the merchandise has been shipped to the customer and the customer has accepted it. Thus, revenue is not realized when a sales contract is made, or when the order is placed, or when the merchandise is manufactured, or when it is paid for; it is realized only when the merchandise is delivered.

The realization principle, like the cost principle, is an effort to make accounting more objective. The accountant says in effect, "It is not until a deal is wrapped up, sealed, and the merchandise or services delivered that I will consider a company to have obtained revenue." Performance, rather than promises, is the guide used for booking revenue under the realization principle.

There is a similarity between the realization principle and the accrual principle. The application of the accrual principle showed that, in accounting, increases or decreases in cash do not necessarily determine the net income of a business. Let's apply the realization principle to Gerry Manero's Furniture Mart.

Assume that on December 31, 19X5, Gerry makes a sale for $200, delivers the merchandise, and receives cash for it the same day. Under the realization concept, since he has delivered the merchandise, he records sales revenues in the amount of $200 and also shows an increase in the cash account of the furniture mart. Both cash and revenue are increased. Later in the day he sells and delivers merchandise for $300. Because he gives the customer credit, however, he does not receive cash until January 19X6. Since he has delivered the merchandise, revenue under the realization principle would be realized (and increased); however, cash remains unchanged. In this instance, revenue is increased; cash, however, is not.

Let's take another example. A customer appears and selects a piece of merchandise and makes full payment of $400 but requests that the merchandise not be delivered until March of the following year. In this case, cash receipts have increased. Because the merchandise is not to be delivered until the following year, however, there is no increase in revenue. A simple table summarizes these three transactions:

GERRY MANERO'S FURNITURE MART
Application of the Realization Principle

Date	Transaction	Amount	Effect on Cash	Effect on Revenue
December 31	Cash sale and delivery same day	$200	$200	$200
December 31	Credit sale and delivery same day	300	0	300
December 31	Payment received in advance for March delivery	400	400	0
	Totals	$900	$600	$500

This table shows that the application of the realization principle may result in situations where the net income of the business can be affected without a corresponding effect on cash.

The realization principle is the last of the basic ideas that form part of our conceptual groundwork. Clearly, accounting principles—unlike mathematical or scientific principles—are by no means scientifically derived. They are agreements between people that have evolved over the years as practical aids to solving accounting problems. Although the use of these accounting principles provides a common and accepted approach to problems associated with the measurement of financial results of a business, there are still an incredible number of ways in which financial results can be presented. Accounting's efforts to cope with this problem are discussed in the next chapter.

4

Accounting Conventions

There is an old story about a successful applicant for the job of chief accountant. After many others had failed to obtain the position, he was hired because he answered the president's question "How much is two and two?" by replying, "How much do you want it to be, sir?"

Businesses also account for their results in a variety of ways. For example, almost all companies can obtain discounts for prompt payment. One company may take these discounts and reduce the cost of merchandise; another may take discounts and record them as revenue or income realized on prompt payments. One company may build a large capital facility and consider the associated costs of its own engineering staff and related corporate efforts as part of the cost of the facility. It may even include in this figure the first four or five months of operation, classifying them as start-up costs. A competitive company, building a similar facility, may ignore these costs and assume that they are expenses chargeable against income for revenues during the period in which they were incurred.

These are but a few of numerous ways in which accounting information can be recorded. What is important to recognize is that exactly the same financial information can be presented many ways, all of them in accordance with the principles we have been discussing. Accounting makes an effort to overcome this deficiency through the use of three so-called accepted, basic accounting conventions: consistency, conservatism, and materiality.

The Convention of Consistency

As its name suggests, the **convention of consistency** says that once a business transaction is accounted for in one particular manner, it must be accounted for in this same way consistently thereafter.

If, for example, a company accounts for cash discounts as revenue or income derived from prompt payments, it must continue to do so in all its succeeding statements of income. This doctrine makes it very difficult for a business to manipulate its figures by showing them on one occasion in a manner that sheds a favorable light on the result and then, when it is convenient, changing to another approach. The convention of consistency is the basis for that portion of the annual audit report of every major publicly held U.S. corporation that reads, in essence, "This statement has been prepared in accordance with generally accepted accounting principles, on a basis *consistent* with the preceding year."

In a more general sense, Emerson once said, "A foolish consistency is the hobgoblin of little minds." In accounting, however, consistency is designed to prevent the manipulation of accounting data from one accounting period to another. This particular convention facilitates the understanding of accounting data, because once a person understands how a particular business transaction is treated in one particular accounting period, he or she can expect it to be treated the same way in subsequent periods.

The Convention of Conservatism

Contrary to what might be expected, the convention of conservatism has nothing to do with how people in the accounting profession dress or behave. We have already discussed the inherently objective and conservative nature of the cost and realization concepts. The convention of conservatism is merely an amplification of the same basic approach. It says that whenever the accountant is given the option to do so, he or she will always choose to reflect financial data in terms of the lower of two possible values.

Perhaps the best example of this occurs in the evaluation of inventories, that is, merchandise held by the company for sale. At the close of the accounting period, the accountant, as we know from the cost concept, values this inventory on the basis of its cost to the business. If, however, its market value at this point is now lower than its original cost, the accountant will, in accordance with the convention of conservatism, reflect the lower value. Accounting statements, without exception, employ this approach in the evaluation of inventories, and it is sometimes called the **cost or market evaluation.** We can see that it grows out of the convention of conservatism.

Another way in which conservatism is commonly applied in accounting practice concerns gains and losses from the sale of property. In this situation, sound accounting invariably recognizes any loss that has occurred or could possibly occur. On the other hand, sound accounting never recognizes profit on the sale of assets until the sale actually takes place.

The major objective of the convention of conservatism, like that of consistency, is to protect the shareholders or owners of a business from a fraudulent or misleading representation of the worth of the business.

The Convention of Materiality

Even though the popular song suggests that "little things mean a lot," they don't to the accountant. This is the essence of the convention of materiality, which says that accounting should not be concerned with immaterial events in the life of a business. But what is "material"? To some of us as individuals, a sum of $2,000 or $3,000 may be quite important and most material, but to any of the corporations in the *Fortune* 500 it is rather insignificant.

The convention of materiality, then, really serves as a philosophical basis for expediency. It says that when a particular transaction is not material to the financial results of the business, the accountant can use his or her own discretion as to when and perhaps how to record that event. The application of the convention of materiality simplifies both the work of the accountant and the structure of his accounting records.

For example, consider the consumption of supplies in the business. Theoretically, each time a piece of paper, a printer ribbon, or a pencil is used, it becomes an expense. As a practical matter, nothing could be more ridiculous (or costly, for that matter) than to account for the expenses of a business with this degree of precision. Obviously, twenty pieces of paper aren't material to the business. Common sense, as well as the convention of materiality, allows the accountant a much more expedient approach. He or she takes only the total costs for the month or even an average of several months' costs of supplies as the expense.

The convention of materiality lies behind the frequent rhetoric in published financial statements that often reads "In the opinion of legal counsel there are no contingencies of material significance," or similar phrasing. Although the convention of materiality serves a highly useful purpose in simplifying the work of the accountant, the user of financial information must be constantly aware that its application is always left to the judgment of the individual accountant. Therefore, when the convention is called into play, the nonfinancial executive should make sure that what is material or immaterial to the accountant is also material or immaterial to the management and the shareholders of a business.

In Chapters 3 and 4 we have covered the fundamental principles and conventions that in combination make up the so-called structural framework of accounting. With this groundwork laid, let us now look in greater depth and detail at the two basic accounting statements: the balance sheet and the income statement.

5

Financial Photography: Balance Sheets and Income Statements

We can think of a business, whether it is a simple proprietorship or a large corporation, as a continuum of business events over a period of time. There are two kinds of events in this continuum. First, there are transactions that change only the status and balance of assets or liabilities. These involve the exchange of one asset for another or an increase in liabilities in exchange for assets. They affect only accounts on a balance sheet and are Balance Sheet transactions. Second, there are transactions that affect the status of assets and liabilities as well as revenue and expense accounts. They are income statement transactions.

Although neither profession may welcome the comparison, it is useful to draw a parallel between the work of the accountant and that of the photographer. Both record events, the photographer with a camera and the accountant with a ledger. We can take the analogy further by thinking of the balance sheet and the income statement as forms of photography, albeit financial photography. Exhibit 5-1 presents this analogy graphically.

In Chapter 1, we looked at the dual aspect concept and its importance to the *theory* of the balance sheet. In developing this concept, we followed on a day-in, day-out basis the events relating to the hypothetical business venture of Gerry Manero. As we de-

Exhibit 5-1. Financial photograph: balance sheet and income statement transactions.

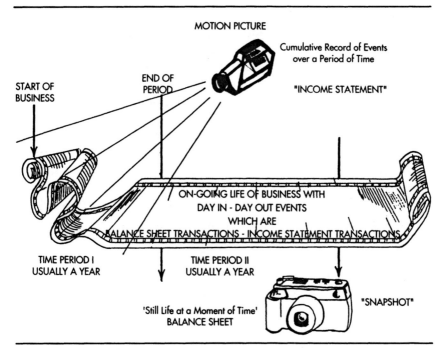

MOTION PICTURE

Cumulative Record of Events over a Period of Time

"INCOME STATEMENT"

START OF BUSINESS

END OF PERIOD

ON-GOING LIFE OF BUSINESS WITH DAY IN - DAY OUT EVENTS WHICH ARE BALANCE SHEET TRANSACTIONS - INCOME STATEMENT TRANSACTIONS

TIME PERIOD I
USUALLY A YEAR

TIME PERIOD II
USUALLY A YEAR

'Still Life at a Moment of Time'
BALANCE SHEET

"SNAPSHOT"

veloped this illustration, we saw that a balance sheet reported the status of a business's assets and liabilities, which were constantly changing. Each day the various items on the balance sheet changed according to that particular day's transactions, and the balance sheet reflected the status of a business's assets and liabilities at only one given moment. For this reason, the balance sheet was always dated.

The similarity between a balance sheet and a photographic snapshot is clear. A snapshot captures a situation only at the moment the picture is taken. Many actions precede the snapshot and others follow it, but the permanent image is the one that remains at the precise moment the photo was snapped. In exactly the same way, many business actions take place before and after the balance sheet is drawn up. The balance sheet in the fancy annual report of a major corporation is something more of a formal portrait, but it remains a still life—a static report on the business at a particular moment.

The income statement, which we discussed in Chapter 2, is similar to another type of photography. The income statement is a mechanism that accumulates the effect of each day's transactions. In the case of Gerry Manero's business, the income statement accumulated the sales for one day, then another, and so on, so that the total sales transacted up to the date the income statement was prepared were reflected in that statement. Thus, an income statement captures and amasses in one record everything that goes on in a business over a period of time. In photography, the form that captures all action and events as they occur and makes a permanent record of them is, of course, the motion picture. In like manner, the income statement permanently records the business actions as they occur during the period in which they are being "photographed" by the accountant.

Our analogy to photography demonstrates some of the basic differences between the income statement and the balance sheet. At the same time, however, it is important to understand clearly the close relationship between them. Let's look again at the balance sheets and income statements we prepared for Gerry Manero. These are given in Exhibit 5-2, which shows that the increase in owner's equity between July 27 and September 15 is exactly the same as the net income on the income statement for the same period.

If Gerry had taken $200 of the net income of the business before preparing the balance sheet on September 15, 19X5, this amount would have had to be reflected in the balance sheet and would have modified the owner's equity section of the balance sheet in this way:

Owner's equity	$600
Less drawings	200
Net owner's equity	$400

Under these circumstances, the increase in owner's equity

Exhibit 5-2. Relationship between balance sheets and income statement for Manero's Furniture Mart.

BALANCE SHEET July 27, 19X5		BALANCE SHEET September 15, 19X5		
Cash	Owner's Equity	Assets		Liabilities and Owner's Equity
$15,000	$15,000	Cash	$10,600	Accounts payable $ 2,000
		Accounts receivable	800	Loans payable 5,000
		Inventory	6,200	Total liabilities $ 7,000
		Delivery truck	5,000	Owner's equity 15,600
		Total	$22,600	Total $22,600

OWNER'S EQUITY

July 27	September 15	Increase
$15,000	$15,600	$600

INCOME STATEMENT
September 15, 19X5

Revenues	$2,400
Less cost of goods sold	1,800
Net increase	$ 600

from one balance sheet to another would be equal to the net income for the period less any net income drawn by Gerry Manero.

The Balance Sheet

With some of these general ideas in mind, let's turn to a more detailed examination of the basic structure and terminology of the balance sheet and the income statement. The balance sheets we have prepared for Gerry Manero have been brief and simple. For a larger, more complex business, they would need to be expanded. Also, the shareholders and the managers of a business are often interested in a greater amount of detail.

Assets

Over a period of time, a standard balance sheet format for the presentation of a business's basic financial data has evolved, in which assets are subdivided into three major categories: **current assets, fixed assets,** and **other assets.**

Current Assets

The five items described below are the most common forms of current assets, although there could be others. Assets are classified as current as long as they are cash, or can be converted into cash, within the customary operating period of the business (usually one year). Current assets, therefore, are cash or assets that can become the equivalent of cash within one year's time.

1. *Cash.* Cash usually represents the funds on hand held by the business, that is, bills or coin and funds that are readily available in checking accounts. It does not include cash funds for which there is some legal constraint against use, such as funds held in special deposits or in escrow.

2. *Marketable securities.* Marketable securities represent temporary investments in the stocks or bonds of other businesses or enterprises and possibly in government bonds. Next to cash, they are usually the most liquid assets and can be turned into cash on short notice.

3. *Accounts receivable.* Accounts receivable represent monies owed to the business by customers for the purchase of merchandise. Accounts receivable are created when goods or services are provided and the business receives a legally enforceable promise of payment rather than cash. In our personal lives, we create accounts receivable whenever we buy merchandise on credit and then wait to make payment on it until we receive a statement of account for the purchase. Accounts receivable are often shown as a gross amount of accounts receivable, and then an "allowance for doubtful accounts" is shown as a deduction. This allowance represents an estimate of accounts receivable on which the business does not expect to be able to collect. (We discuss the account-

ing of doubtful accounts receivable in more detail in subsequent chapters.)

4. *Inventories.* Inventories represent merchandise that has been purchased by a business and is being held in stock until such time as it is resold. Gerry Manero's Furniture Mart is an example of this type of inventory. When a business manufactures its own product for sale, inventories include the value of the merchandise or product that has been manufactured and is being held in readiness for sale. Moreover, such a business often needs raw materials from which to make the product. Also, at any given time certain products are in the process of being manufactured. Both of these inventories are made in addition to the finished products inventory. Many manufacturing companies often show their inventories in this order: raw material inventories, goods in process inventories, and finished goods inventories.

5. *Prepaid expenses.* Prepaid expenses are those that have been paid in advance by the business. They constitute a right to a future service that will be used but that has not yet been used by the business. A common example of a prepaid expense is the insurance coverage a business pays for in advance of receiving services.

Fixed Assets

Fixed assets consist of tangible permanent investments in so-called capital facilities, usually brick and mortar, or equipment. In many balance sheets, these particular assets are much more descriptively and accurately labeled **property, plant, and equipment.**

Almost all these fixed assets are shown in the following order in the balance sheet: gross fixed assets, accumulated depreciation, and net fixed assets.

The term **gross fixed assets** refers to the original value, that is, the cost incurred to purchase or construct the physical facility (note the application of the cost concept). Gross fixed assets are reduced by an item called **accumulated depreciation.** Depreciation is a major accounting concept in itself, which we shall discuss in detail in subsequent chapters. At this point, let us define depreciation as an estimate of how much the original value of all the company's assets have decreased owing to usage, passage of time, obsolescence, or a combination of these. This amount is deducted from the gross fixed assets to arrive at the figure for net fixed assets, which is the value (that is, the cost) of the fixed assets diminished by the depreciation that has accumulated to the date of the financial statement.

Other Assets

Other assets, the third and final classification of assets on the balance sheet, include various assets that cannot readily be classified as either current or fixed. Other assets, like fixed assets, tend to be long term. The most common of these is **investments.** A company can have marketable securities that are also investments. Investments shown under this heading usually differ in several respects from marketable securities. First, they are intended to be held for an extended period of time—at least one year or longer. Second, they are being held to control the company owned or to earn a significant return on the holding, or both.

Intangible assets are another common form of other assets. They include patents, copyrights, franchises, and similar matters. These assets can have a significant value in generating income for the business, but they are distinct in their form from the tangibility of, say, a plant.

Liabilities and Shareholders' Equities

The right side of the balance sheet consists of the claims on the assets of a corporation. These are: (1) liabilities, which are the claims of the creditors, and (2) the claims of the owners, which are owner's equities. The liabilities and owner's equities sections of a balance sheet are also broken down to standard subclassifications: current liabilities, long-term liabilities, and shareholders' equity.

Current Liabilities

Current liabilities include obligations that are expected to fall due within the next accounting period (usually the next year).

This particular definition corresponds to the same time parameter used in the definition of current assets. There are several types of common current liabilities.

Accounts payable represent the counterpart of accounts receivable. With an account payable, the business is a debtor rather than a creditor. Thus, it has a legal obligation to make a payment rather than to receive it.

Notes payable are similar to accounts payable. Usually the legal instrument associated with this obligation is much more formal and involves a longer period of time for payment. A note payable, like an account payable, has its converse in the note receivable, which is shown on the left side of the balance sheet as an asset.

Under law, the term **accrue** means to become a present right or enforceable demand. In accounting, the term is used similarly, and **accrued liabilities** represent obligations of the business that have not yet been paid. Such obligations can take several forms and may or may not be indicated separately on the balance sheet. One of the most common to be shown separately is accrued taxes, which can include federal, state, or local income taxes, as well as real estate taxes. Another customary type of accrued liability is wages and salaries owed to workers and employees for services they have already provided to the business.

Long-Term Liabilities

Long-term liabilities include those debts (or claims on assets) that fall due a year or further in the future. Long-term liabilities are usually incurred to obtain more permanent funds for the business. They are often shown according to the source of funds.

Funds obtained from bank loans can be either a short- or long-term liability. If they are due and payable within one year from the date of the balance sheet, they are classified as a short-term liability. If they are payable in more than a year, they are classified as a long-term liability and are shown in this section of the balance sheet.

Bonds, another form of long-term capital, are loans that are often obtained from many people who are given certificates, called bonds, as evidence of the loan. Bonds usually have extended 15- to 20-year repayment periods.

Shareholders' Equity

The lower left section of the balance sheet contains the shareholders' (or owner's) equity section. Shareholders' equities, as we have discussed, represent the claim the owners have on the assets of the business after the obligations to all other creditors have been fulfilled. There are usually two basic forms of shareholders' equity.

Common stock (or capital stock) represents the original contribution to the business that has been made by the owners. In the case of an individual proprietorship, such as that of Gerry Manero, this contribution represents the original amount of the funds put into the business. In the case of a corporation, the contribution may be a large number of shares that have been sold to thousands of individual investors through an established public stock exchange. Under any form of business structure, these are the funds originally contributed by the owners of the business. They are to be used to purchase assets and conduct the affairs subsequent to formation of the business.

Retained earnings is the second classification under shareholders' equity. The retained earnings of the business represent the total cumulative net income that a business earns over its life, less any funds that have been returned to the owners in the form of dividends. We showed the buildup of retained earnings for a period of one year for Gerry Manero in Exhibit 5-2.

In the past, the term **earned surplus** was frequently used to describe the retained earnings of a business. In some instances, this phrase is still used. However, it is appropriately falling into disuse, since "surplus" is misleading. The funds are not surplus, because they have been ploughed back into the business to provide monies for expansion and growth.

The Income Statement

In the early stages of the development of U.S. industry, assets tended to be the determining factor in the worth of a business.

Exhibit 5-3. A typical income statement for the year ended 19X6.

Sales	$3,100,000
Less cost of goods sold	2,350,000
Gross profit	$ 750,000
Less operating expenses	
Selling expenses	250,000
Administration expenses	200,000
Operating profit	$ 300,000
Provision for income taxes	144,000
Net income	$ 156,000

For this reason, investors' and shareholders' attention focused primarily on a company's balance sheet. Times have changed, however, and investors now emphasize the so-called growth potential of the corporation. Generally, this is the ability of a corporation to sustain a constantly increasing rate of growth in net income year after year.

This change has switched attention from the balance sheet to the income statement. Let's look at a typical income statement, as shown in Exhibit 5-3.

Sales

The first item on this income statement is **sales.** Sometimes this item is called sales revenue or just revenue, but, whatever its title, it refers to the amounts received (or to be received—accounts receivable) for goods or services provided (or, under the realization principle, delivered) to other organizations in the conduct of its business for the period shown, in our example, during 19X6.

Cost of Goods Sold

The second item on the income statement is **cost of goods sold.** As in our illustration, it is usually shown as **less cost of goods**

sold since it is deducted from sales. The term had the same meaning when we used it to prepare Gerry Manero's income statement. It represents what it cost the business to either purchase or manufacture the goods it has sold in order to generate the revenues that appear in the first line, sales. In most businesses, other than those providing a service, cost of goods sold represents the most significant item of expense for the business. For this reason, it is almost always shown as a separate item.

Gross Profit

The subtraction of cost of goods sold from sales leaves a remainder called **gross profit,** the third item on the income statement. Gross profit is almost invariably shown as a separate item on an income statement. It indicates the income that remains to cover the expenses of selling the product and administering the business.

Operating Expenses

The next item on the income statement is called **operating expenses,** which are the expenses incurred to operate the business for the period covered by the income statement. Sometimes they are shown as a single item or subdivided, as in our illustration, into the two major components, selling expenses and administrative expenses. Selling expenses include the cost of sales organization, sales promotions, and similar factors. Administrative expenses cover the cost of managing the organization and typically include insurance costs, rent, heat, light, accounting, and legal costs.

Operating Profit

Operating expenses reduce the amount of the company's gross profit and must be covered before net income can be generated. The deduction of operating expenses from gross profit leaves the business's **operating profit,** which is shown as another separate subtotal and represents profit that has been provided from the normal operations of the business. Many income statements make a distinction between operating and nonoperating profits in order to differentiate the net income generated as a result of the normal routine conduct of the business from the net income generated by sale of equipment or property or some other, similar transaction not normally considered the basic function of the business. Sometimes operating profit is described as **net income before taxes.**

Income Taxes

The next item on the income statement is **provision for income taxes.** Income taxes, which have become a significant item for reducing business income, are almost always shown separately.

Net Income

The final line on the income statement, **net income,** is, of course, the most critical piece of information, the final net result of operating the business for the period covered by the income statement. Net income, as we have stressed before, represents the increment (or if there is a net loss, the decrement) that has resulted from successful operation of the business for the period of time covered by the income statement.

Balance sheets and income statements are the output of accounting systems. We turn next to a more detailed discussion of certain special accounting problems and concepts involved in obtaining this output.

6

Special Accounting Problems

In this chapter, we look at three special accounting problems: (1) fixed assets accounting, which includes depreciation costs; (2) inventory accounting, which is the cost of goods sold determination; and (3) accounts receivable, which is accounting for bad debts.

These three areas are given special attention for two reasons. First, they involve some concepts, procedures, and terminology that are critical to the proper understanding and utilization of financial data. Second, they include areas that the nonfinancial executive often finds troublesome and difficult to understand.

Fixed Assets

In Chapter 4, we defined fixed assets as permanent investments of a long-term nature in so-called capital facilities. These include property, plant, and equipment that will be used by the business to provide goods or services.

Recording Original Value

The first logical question concerning fixed asset accounting is: On what basis should their value be recorded? The application of the cost principle gives the answer to this question—which is cost.

The next question then becomes: Exactly what makes up the cost? The answer has become well defined in accounting practice and can be summarized as follows:

1. The cost of fixed assets includes all costs of obtaining and installing the fixed assets. For example, assume that a business purchases a piece of land for $50,000. There is a $3,000 payment to the real estate agent along with a $1,500 fee to the lawyer for the closing. Finally, there is a cost of $1,500 for clearing and filing the property. In this instance, the cost of the fixed asset includes all these costs because they were required to make the facility ready for use by the business.

Another example could be the purchase of a piece of machinery, with the cost of transportation and installation included in the fixed cost. Thus, the basic cost of the machinery might be $1,000, but there could be an additional $200 installation cost and a $100 freight charge. Then the total cost of the fixed asset would be recorded on the books as $1,300.

2. A business may construct a machine or a building, using its own labor, or some of its own labor, for the partial construction or installation. The costs the company incurs for this labor are included as part of the asset.

3. A business may acquire a new asset, the payment of which is made partly in cash and partly in the value of the old assets traded in. For example, if a business buys a calculating machine for $500 cash with a trade-in value of $300 for the old machine, the total real cost of the new calculating machine is $800, not $500, and $800 is the figure used to record the total cost of the asset.

Depreciation

We have said that fixed assets include property, plant, and equipment that will be used by the business to provide goods or services. The buildings, equipment, and machinery used for this purpose day after day will obviously wear out and ultimately become useless. As this process takes place, the original value of the asset decreases, with a corresponding reduction in the owner's equity. To illustrate this process, let's trace an example in a series of simplified balance sheets.

Event. A delivery service is started with a $5,000 purchase of delivery truck by the owner.

**Balance Sheet
Delivery Service
Beginning of Year**

Assets		*Equities*	
Fixed assets	$5,000	Owner's equity	$5,000

Event. Delivery service is operated for a year, but the truck now has less value, since it is older and has been used. The truck now has a value of only $3,500.

**Balance Sheet
Delivery Service
End of Year**

Assets		*Equity*	
Fixed assets	$3,500	Owner's equity	$3,500

In this example, reduction in the asset value has been taken as a direct deduction to owner's equity. We know, however, that under regular procedures this decrease would be shown by reflecting the amount as an expense (which is also a reduction of owner's equity) in an income statement. The process of taking the estimated usage of an asset each year and charging it as an expense against the business is called **depreciation.**

The more technologically oriented a business is, the more important the factor of obsolescence becomes, although depreciation includes the effect of both factors. We should clarify, however, that not all fixed assets are depreciated. Fixed assets include land as well as plant and equipment. The value of land tends to be permanent. When it is used as a building site (other than being mined or farmed), it does not wear out. In fact, it tends to appreciate in value. For these reasons the accountant does not depreciate land.

Other types of fixed assets do wear out, and to calculate the expense associated with this process of depreciation, the accountant has to determine three facts:

1. The original cost of the asset, which is usually determined in accordance with the principles set forth at the outset of this chapter.
2. The estimated life of the asset.
3. The estimated residual or scrap value, if any, of the asset at the end of its life.

Let's apply these three factors to determine the depreciation of a fixed asset, remembering that our objective is to determine the estimated usage of the asset and to record it as an expense during the period when it is used to produce revenues for the business.

Assume that a business purchases a machine with a basic factory cost of $1,000, and there are also $100 of costs to deliver it and another $100 to install it on the premises. Applying the guidelines we have just discussed, we can readily determine that the total original cost of the fixed asset is $1,200.

The next step is to determine the estimated salvage value. Almost all machinery has some residual value—when it is disposed of. The word "estimated" here is critical because, of course, this can be nothing more than an educated guess as to what the machine will be worth at the time of disposal. Although this is a difficult guess to make, it is by no means impossible. Let's assume that on the basis of past experience and/or consultation with used-machinery dealers, the accountant concludes that the final estimated salvage value of the machinery will be $200. Now that we have the original cost of the fixed asset as well as the estimated salvage value, we can determine the estimated net cost of the asset, which is simply the difference between these two—in our case, $1,000.

The next step is to determine the estimated useful life. There are a variety of sources from which the accountant can obtain the estimated useful life. One of the most common is the guidelines issued by the Internal Revenue Service. Others are engineering and equipment manufacturers. Assume that we arrive at an estimate of four years. We now have all three elements we need to arrive at our estimated annual depreciation expense, which we can calculate to be $250 per year. This is obtained by dividing the estimated net cost of the fixed asset, that is, the original $1,200

Exhibit 6-1. Straight-line depreciation.

of cost less the estimated salvage value of $200, by the useful life period of four years, as shown below:

Purchase price of asset	$1,000
Delivery cost	100
Installation cost	100
Total cost of asset	$1,200
Less estimated salvage value	200
Asset cost to be depreciated	$1,000

$$\frac{\$1{,}000 \text{ (asset cost to be depreciated)}}{4 \text{ years}} = \$250 \text{ per year}$$

If we were to plot this process graphically, it would appear as shown in Exhibit 6-1.

Because the process of depreciating the estimated net cost of the fixed asset in equal annual amounts of depreciation expense results in a straight line, this technique for determining depreciation expense is called the **straight-line method of depreciation.** It is simple in both conception and application and is the most commonly used approach in U.S. business. Applying this method, the resulting usage cost or depreciation expense becomes the same for each year of the estimated useful life of the asset. For example, an asset with a net asset value of $1,000 with an estimated useful life of ten years would have a yearly amount of $100 expensed as depreciation each year.

In real life, however, assets do not always necessarily wear out or obsolesce at the same rate each year. The straight-line method of depreciation ignores this fact. As an everyday example of this phenomenon, consider your own automobile, on which the obsolescence factor is much more pronounced in the earlier years of ownership and operation. The same holds true in many business situations.

For this reason, three different so-called accelerated methods of depreciation have been developed and are now accepted accounting practice. Unlike the straight-line method, which takes equal annual amounts for usage, accelerated methods take more of the expense for the usage of the asset at the beginning of its life than at the end. There are three accelerated methods of depreciation, which are described below.

Sum of the Years Digits

The formula for calculating sum-of-the-years-digits depreciation is a fraction, with the numerator representing the years of remaining useful life of the asset and the denominator indicating the sum of the digits of the years of estimated useful life. Using this approach, we would depreciate the machine with a net asset value of $1,000 in the following way:

1. Calculate the sum of the digits of the years of estimated useful life; that is, 4 years = 1 + 2 + 3 + 4 = 10.
2. Determine depreciation to be taken in each year, starting in the first year, for the number of years of remaining useful life.

		Rate			
Year of Life	Years Remaining	Fraction		Percent	Depreciation
1	4	$4/10$	=	40	$ 400
2	3	$3/10$	=	30	300
3	2	$2/10$	=	20	200
4	1	$1/10$	=	10	100
10	10			100	$1,000

Double Declining Balance

The first step in the double-declining-balance method is to determine the rate of depreciation by means of the straight-line method. This figure is then doubled, and then always taken on the declining balance of the value of the asset. The following steps illustrate the double-declining-balance method, again using the machine with a net asset value of $1,000 as an example.

1. Determine rate of depreciation under straight-line method; that is, four years or 25%.
2. Double rate of depreciation used under straight-line method; that is, 25% × 2 = 50%.
3. Apply rate, always using the declining balance of net asset as the value.

Year	Value	Rate (%)	Depreciation	Declining Value
1	$1,000.00	50	$500.00	$500.00
2	500.00	50	250.00	250.00
*3	250.00	50	125.00	125.00
*4	125.00	50	125.00	0

* Note: Under most cases, the total depreciation would not be allocated during the life of the asset. Therefore, at a period where the amount that each period of depreciation is below the straight-line amount (in this example, $250), the remaining underdepreciated value ($250) is calculated on a straight-line basis (in this example $125 each accounting period) over the remaining life of the asset (2 years).

Units of Activity Method

Another method used expresses units of activity as a base instead of time. This method is referred to as the units of activity method.

This method uses total units of production expected from the asset, rather than a period of time. It is an ideal method to use in a factory, where production can be measured, or in cases where activity can be measured in miles, as for a vehicle.

Using the set of facts already given but substituting the units of activity for the depreciable rate percentage, the following annual depreciation can be calculated.

Let's assume that the machine is estimated to have life of 8,000 units and with the following yearly estimates:

Year 1:	1,200 units
Year 2:	2,500 units
Year 3:	1,600 units
Year 4:	2,000 units
Year 5:	700 units

since the depreciable cost of the asset is $1,000 and the total of units of activity is 8,000 units, the depreciation cost per unit is $0.125 ($1,000/8,000 units). Multiplying the depreciation cost per unit by the yearly unit activity yields the following annual depreciation expense.

Year	Units of Activity	×	Depreciation Cost Per Unit	=	Annual Depreciation
1	1,200		$0.125		$ 150.00
2	2,500		0.125		312.50
3	1,600		0.125		200.00
4	2,000		0.125		250.00
5	700		0.125		87.50
	8,000				$1,000.00

Comparison of Methods

A comparison of the four methods is summarized below.

Year	Straight-Line	Sum of the Years Digits	Declining Balance	Units of Activity
1	$ 250	$ 400	$ 500	$ 150.00
2	250	300	250	312.50
3	250	200	125	200.00
4	250	100	125	250.00
5				87.50
	$1,000	$1,000	$1,000	$1,000.00

Since different methods of depreciation can be used in preparing tax returns and accounting statements, many companies choose to use straight-line depreciation in calculating their financial statements to maximize net income. On the other hand, some companies use an accelerated method in preparing tax returns to minimize their income tax obligations.

Accumulated Depreciation

In accounting, the assets of a business are subject to an invariable life cycle. As they are used to generate revenues for the business, they become an expense. Thus, cash may be used to pay a salesperson who is generating revenue through his or her selling efforts. The asset of cash decreases, and the expense of selling increases.

Merchandise inventory is an asset. When the merchandise is sold, the asset inventory decreases, and the expense of cost of goods sold increases.

The prepayment of insurance premiums results in an asset, prepaid expenses. As this insurance coverage is utilized with the passage of time, however, the asset of prepaid insurance decreases, and the expense of insurance increases.

In accounting for fixed assets, we follow this same approach. Since the fixed asset is consumed in the life of the business, the cost of its usage is taken as an expense called depreciation. The time period involved is longer, and estimates must be made, but the basic procedure, as in all other cases, is to decrease the asset as it is used and to increase the expense.

There is one additional difference: The value of the fixed asset on the balance sheet is not reduced directly, as was the case with other forms of assets. Instead, the accountant accumulates these reductions in a special account so that they can be shown separately on the balance sheet. This special account is called **accumulated depreciation.** As depreciation expense is incurred, the accountant increases this cumulative account (sometimes called a contra account) and at the same time increases the item of depreciation expense that appears in the income statement.

The purpose behind this process is to allow fixed assets always to appear on the balance sheet at their original gross value. The extent to which they have been used can then be determined from the accumulated depreciation account in order to arrive at the estimated net fixed value of the assets. This procedure provides more information to the reader of the financial statement. Fixed assets stay on the balance sheet even though they may be 100 percent depreciated. Thus, it is possible for fixed assets to appear on a balance sheet in the following manner:

Fixed Assets	
Gross (property, plant, and equipment)	$283,000
Less accumulated depreciation	282,000
	$ 1,000

At the time a fixed asset is actually disposed of, the gain or loss on its sale is shown as a nonoperating profit or loss in the income statement. If the fixed asset is sold at an amount greater than originally estimated as its salvage value, there is a gain. If it is sold at an amount less, there is a loss.

Inventory Accounting

Let us turn now to the second special problem area—inventory accounting, which is concerned with the asset item of inventories and the expense factor of cost of goods sold. Earlier we defined the cost of goods sold as the cost of the product purchased for resale and/or manufactured for sale to obtain revenue. The cost of goods sold, except in the case of service industries, is by far the largest element of cost in an income statement and is therefore one of the most important items of expense. Since the accountant must always try to match expenses with revenues, only the costs of the goods that have been sold to generate sales revenue is included in the cost of the goods sold for the period.

Perpetual Inventory Accounting Procedures

In some businesses the process of determining the cost of goods sold is relatively easy. Take, for example, a yacht dealer. Because he has very few sales, his inventory accounting problems are simple. He has little trouble keeping track of what he buys and sells. When he purchases a yacht for cash, he exchanges one asset (cash) for another (inventory). When the yacht is sold again for cash, these things happen: (1) his asset of cash increases, (2) his revenue increases at the same time, (3) his asset of inventory decreases, and (4) his expense of cost of goods sold increases. Thus, if the yacht in question cost $100,000 and is sold for $120,000, the net result is net income of $20,000.

When a business has a limited number of sales, but they are of a high value, the accountant can easily and practically maintain a record of each individual item in inventory and easily determine the value of inventories and the cost of goods sold. This approach is called **perpetual inventory accounting,** and although it's simple, it's practical only for low-volume, high-price businesses where each sale represents a significant part of revenue.

Deductive Inventory Accounting Procedures

By way of contrast, think of a common discount store or supermarket where for most of the day literally thousands of transactions take place. Cash registers ring constantly as customers check out and leave the store with merchandise. The perpetual inventory accounting practices that are used by the yacht dealer are impossible in this situation. The cost of goods sold must be deduced. This can easily be done as long as the following information is available: goods on hand at the beginning of a period, goods purchased during the period, and goods on hand at the end of the period.

Information concerning the goods on hand at the beginning and the end of the period can be obtained simply by taking a physical count of the merchandise and valuing it on the basis of the price at which it was purchased. The value of the goods purchased during the period can be obtained from records maintained for this purpose. As an illustration, assume the records of a discount store show the following:

Goods on hand, March 31, 19XI	$10,000
Purchases during April 19XI	13,000
Goods on hand, April 30, 19XI	7,000

From these facts we can conclude that the $10,000 of merchandise on hand at the beginning of April, together with the $13,000 purchased during April, gave us total goods available for sale of $23,000 during April. If at the end of April, $7,000 of goods were on hand, then $16,000 worth of goods must have been sold during that month.

A more conventional, formal accounting presentation of these same facts would appear as follows:

Beginning inventory, April 1, 19XI	$10,000
Purchases	13,000
Goods available	$23,000
Less closing inventory	7,000
Cost of goods sold	$16,000

The closing inventory for one period must, of course, be the beginning inventory for the subsequent period. The closing inventory value used in the formula to deduce cost of goods sold is the same one shown as the asset of inventory on the balance sheet.

Using this approach, the determination of cost of goods sold involved the use of deductive inventory accounting procedures. These procedures are a practical way to account for the cost of goods sold for businesses that have a high-volume and/or a low-value sales pattern. It is important to recognize that in deducing the cost of goods sold, an implicit procedural assumption is made that the merchandise has actually been sold. This may not always be the case, for in fact there may have been shrinkage, spoilage, or even pilferage of the merchandise. The user of accounting data should always bear this possibility in mind when looking at the accountant's cost of goods sold.

Inventory Valuation

Deductive and perpetual inventory accounting procedures provide the accountant with two different methods to use to tally, or register, business inventories and to obtain the cost of goods sold. Additional complexities can be, and often are, associated with the inventory valuation process.

Let's take as an example Gerry Manero's brother, who is the owner of a service station. He, like Gerry, is preparing accounting records for his business. At the end of April he deduced his cost of goods sold in accordance with that date:

INVENTORIES NO-LEAD GASOLINE

	No. of Gallons	Price per Gallon	Value
Opening inventory, April 1	10,000	$1.20	$12,000
Purchases in April	12,000	1.20	14,400
Goods available	22,000		26,400
Less ending inventory, April 30	8,000		9,600
Cost of goods sold for April	14,000		$16,800

There is no problem here. However, in the following month the cost he had to pay for gasoline increased 3 cents a gallon. Data for the month of May appeared as shown below:

INVENTORIES NO-LEAD GASOLINE

	No. of Gallons	Price per Gallon	Value
Opening inventory, May 1	8,000	$1.20	$ 9,600
Purchases in May	10,000	1.23	12,300
Goods available	18,000		$21,900
Less inventory, May 31	10,000		
Cost of goods sold for May	8,000		

As a result of the price change, we now have a problem finding the value of the closing inventory. By deduction, we know that during the month of May Gerry's brother sold 8,000 gallons of gasoline. What we don't know is whether they were bought at the new price of $1.23 a gallon or at the old price of $1.20 a gallon. All the gallons are in the same tank and physically indistinguishable from each other, so the answer is by no means clear-cut. The dilemma is placed squarely in the lap of the accountant. He or she can resolve this particular problem in one of several ways.

First, he or she can make a so-called FIFO assumption. FIFO is an acronym for **first in, first out.** FIFO assumes that goods that enter into an inventory first are sold first. If in our particular illustration the accountant were to employ the FIFO assumption, the May valuation of inventories and cost of goods sold for Gerry's brother would appear as follows:

INVENTORIES NO-LEAD GASOLINE
FIFO APPROACH

	No. of Gallons	Price per Gallon	Value
Opening inventory, May 1	8,000	$1.20	$ 9,600
Purchases in May	10,000	1.23	12,300
Goods available	18,000		$21,900
Less ending inventory, May 31	10,000	1.23	12,300
Cost of goods sold for May	8,000	$1.20	$ 9,600

Under the FIFO assumption, the most current purchases, that is, those made at $1.23 per gallon, are shown as part of the inventory rather than as the cost of goods sold during the accounting period.

A second alternate approach the accountant can employ is LIFO, which stands for **last in, first out.** The LIFO approach is exactly the opposite of the FIFO approach. It assumes that the most recent purchases are the ones that have been sold and values the goods shown in inventory at the older purchase cost. Under LIFO, the inventory calculation in our example would be changed as follows:

INVENTORIES NO-LEAD GASOLINE
LIFO APPROACH

	No. of Gallons	Price per Gallon	Value
Opening inventory, May 1	8,000	$1.20	$ 9,600
Purchases in May	10,000	1.23	12,300
Goods available	18,000		$21,900
Less ending inventory, May 31	10,000*		12,060
Cost of goods sold for May	8,000	$1.23	$ 9,840

* Made up of 2,000 gallons at $1.23 = $2,460 and 8,000 gallons at $1.20 = $9,600.

A third alternative is the **average method,** under which the account simply averages the costs of the opening inventory and purchases and then the cost of the goods sold for the period at this average. Under this approach we would have the following:

INVENTORIES NO-LEAD GASOLINE
FIFO APPROACH

	No. of Gallons	Price per Gallon	Value
Opening inventory, May 1	8,000	$1.20	$ 9,600
Purchases in May	10,000	1.23	12,300
Goods available	18,000		$21,900
Less ending inventory, May 31	10,000	1.217	12,170
Cost of goods sold for May	8,000		$ 9,730

* Derived: $21,900 ÷ 18,000 gallons = $1.2166 per gallon rounded off to $1.217 per gallon.

It is important to recognize that the accountant's choice of method has an influence on the financial results for the period. A comparison of the gross profit from the sale of no-lead gasoline for May under the three inventory valuation methods gives these results:

NO-LEAD GASOLINE
GROSS PROFIT COMPARISON

	LIFO	FIFO	Average
Sales: 8,000 gallons @ $1.30	$10,400	$10,400	$10,400
Less cost of goods sold	9,840	9,600	9,730
Gross profit	$ 560	$ 800	$ 670
Inventory value to be shown on blance sheet	$12,060	$12,300	$12,170

Under the LIFO approach, the cost of goods sold is higher than it is under either the FIFO or the average method. As a consequence, profits are lower.

The costs of services and materials in the United States have clearly been increasing. When this happens, the use of LIFO inventory evaluation methods tends to lower net income. Since lower net income results in lower tax payments to the United States government, it has been very much in the interest of business to use the LIFO method of inventory evaluation, and it is a commonly used method in U.S. business today. The important fact for the nonfinancial executive to appreciate, however, is that the accountant does have options and that the method he chooses can have a significant influence on the so-called final net book results of the business.

Accounts Receivable

We turn now to the final special accounting problem, which is accounts receivable. Almost all businesses must sell on credit. When they do, they receive an account receivable (a legal obligation to be paid) in lieu of cash. Accounts receivable appear on the balance sheet as assets. If for some reason the account receivable cannot be collected, it has no value. Fortunately, most accounts receivable are collected, and, in fact, sound credit practices should prevent a business from selling on credit to anyone from whom it doesn't think it can collect. Despite these precautions, every business ends up with some uncollectable accounts. Various accounting methods are used to deal with this particular aspect of business life.

The most direct approach is simply to write off a bad debt once it becomes clear that payment will not be received. When this is done, the accountant reduces the value of accounts receivable by the amount of the write-off and increases the expense, and the uncollected payment is called a **bad debt**. The problem with this approach is that the accountant has to wait for an actual bad debt loss to transpire before it can be recognized. In the interim, however, the asset of accounts receivable is not shown in either the most realistic or the most conservative manner, since it is a known fact that all the accounts receivable won't be collected. What is not known is who won't pay and the amounts. To overcome this problem, the general practice is to make a comprehensive estimate of the total amount of accounts receivable that won't be collected. This estimate is called an **allowance for doubtful accounts**. This allowance is taken as a reduction from the accounts receivable on the balance sheet and usually appears as shown:

Accounts receivable	$200,000
Less allowance for doubtful accounts	7,000
	$193,000

At the same time the allowance for doubtful accounts is created and used to decrease the value of the asset, a corresponding increase occurs in the expense—bad debts.

The actual amount that is to be set up as allowance for doubtful accounts is usually based on the company's past experience. Management may determine that a certain percentage of the annual net sales, say 2 to 3 percent, is appropriate. Alternately, it may make a similar determination on the basis of only its credit sales. When this is done, the allowance is reflected in the balance sheet, as was shown.

On the occasion of an actual bad debt write-off, both the asset of accounts receivable and the allowance are reduced by the amount of the write-off. If we assume a write-off of $1,000, the figures just shown would be modified as follows:

	Before Write-off	After Write-off
Accounts receivable	$200,000	$199,000
Less allowance for doubtful accounts	7,000	6,000
	$193,000	$193,000

Accounting for fixed assets, inventory, cost of goods sold, and bad debts involves the nonfinancial executive in some special problems and aspects of the accounting process. This chapter has attempted to demonstrate that the methods and techniques used by accountants are less difficult and enigmatic than they may seem and that it is important for the nonfinancial executive to understand them.

7

The Basic Accounting
Process

Although the primary purpose of this book is to show how to use rather than how to create accounting data, we cannot ignore the latter aspect altogether nor, in fact, should we do so. The nonfinancial executive needs to have at least an elementary understanding of the basic accounting process.

Up to this point, we have described the effect of business transactions simply in terms of increases or decreases in assets, liabilities, and so on. In Chapters 1 and 2 we traced the development of Gerry Manero's Furniture Mart by actually changing the balance sheet for the business with each transaction. Although this approach was helpful as background, use of this method to account for the business activities of an enterprise of any size would be impractical to the point of impossibility.

More than two centuries ago, merchants devised a much more practical method of double-entry accounting. The effects of business transactions are collected in records called accounts. The simplest form of an account is the so-called T account, which, as the name suggests, looks like this:

Every item of financial information that appears on the balance sheet and the income statement has an account. In all likelihood, there will be many subaccounts for each item; these are "rolled up" and shown as only one figure on a financial statement. The accountant can create an account for any particular item of information he or she wants to know about the business. For example, he or she may want to know not only total sales but sales by types of customers such as government, manufacturers, wholesalers, agents, or retailers. To capture this information, he or she sets up subaccounts under the general sales account. The constraint on setting up accounts, of course, is the increase in the cost and complexity of the accounting system. But no matter how many accounts are set up, they always conform to the general framework of a balance sheet and an income statement. Thus, asset, liability, and owner's equity accounts appear on the balance sheet, and revenue, expense, and net income are shown on the income statement.

Basic Rules of the Accounting Process

The accounting process involves some basic rules under which accounting data is recorded.

1. *Entry.* The recording of a business transaction in an account is referred to as an **accounting entry.**

2. *Debits and Credits.* An entry on the left side of an account is called a **debit.** An entry on the right side is called a **credit.** Graphically, this appears in a T form:

T Account	
Debit	Credit
Entry on left side	Entry on right side

When the terms "debit" and "credit" are used in the accounting process, they have no meaning other than the above. This is an important point for the reader to recognize, since "credit" frequently has other connotations. These should be ignored when working with the term in accounting.

Balance sheet and income statement accounts increase and decrease with debits and credits in accordance with the following immutable rules:

Balance Sheet Accounts

Assets
- Debit entries increase an asset account.
- Credit entries decrease an asset account.

Liabilities
- Debit entries decrease a liability account.
- Credit entries increase a liability account.

Owner's Equity
- Debit entries decrease owner's equity accounts.
- Credit entries increase owner's equity accounts.

Income Statement Accounts

Revenue
- Debit entries decrease revenue accounts.
- Credit entries increase revenue accounts.

Expenses
- Debit entries increase expense accounts.
- Credit entries decrease expense accounts.

Net Income
- Debit entries decrease net income accounts.
- Credit entries increase net income accounts.

These rules are summarized graphically in T account form in Exhibit 7-1, which shows clearly the logic of the debit-credit mechanism of the accounting process. Note, for example, the relationship between the effects of debits and credits in owner's equity accounts and income statement accounts. Owner's equity increases with credits. Revenue, which benefits owner's equity, also increases with credit.

Expenses, we have said, decrease owner's equity. This is shown by debiting the owner's equity account. An increase in expenses is also shown by debiting the expense account.

Exhibit 7-1. Double-entry accounting formula.

BALANCE SHEET ACCOUNTS

Assets		Liabilities	
Dr.	Cr.	Dr.	Cr.
+	–	–	+

	Owner's Equity	
	Dr.	Cr.
	–	+

INCOME STATEMENT ACCOUNTS

Revenue		Expenses	
Dr.	Cr.	Dr.	Cr.
–	+	+	–

	Net Income	
	Dr.	Cr.
	–	+

Key
+ = increase
– = decrease

In previous chapters, we showed that assets decrease as they are consumed and that, through the process of becoming an expense, they reduce owner's equity. Exhibit 7-1 shows how this occurs through a credit entry to reduce the asset and a debit entry to increase expense (or reduce owner's equity).

Despite the logic of the debit-credit formula, most people (including many practicing accountants) usually find it considerably more practical simply to commit the formula to memory than to think through the logic of every accounting transaction. It is rumored that many a competent accountant has more than once referred to a secret formula: "The debits are by the window, the credits are by the door."*

A final point, which will not come as a surprise, is that all accounting entries must balance. That is, the debits must always equal the credits. Each particular entry may include two or three elements, but they must in the final sum always be equal to the corresponding debit or credit. This is in keeping with the concept of the balance sheet, which requires that assets and equities always be in balance.

Filing Systems

Two instruments are used to file and record accounting data. One of these is the accounting ledger. We've already discussed the concept of an account. When all the accounts a business uses are grouped together, it is called a ledger; hence the familiar term "company ledger."

The accounting journal is the other method. A journal is a log, a document used to record on a daily basis the events that take place. In accounting, the journal is the daily record of the transactions (or events) that occur in the business. Unlike the traveler, who writes in everyday English about the sights and events of his trip, the accountant records his or her entries in his or her own particular language of debits and credits. For example, assume that on any given day, just after Gerry Manero has opened his furniture mart, a customer appears and pays a bill. To record this event in the journal, the accountant would indicate that the business's cash account had increased and that the accounts receivable from customers had decreased. Using the language of debits and credits, he or she would make an entry in a journal book that would appear as follows:

> *Debit* Cash
> *Credit* Accounts receivable

The accountant usually abbreviates the entry in the following form:

---

* Debits are on the left side and credits are on the right side of the equation.

> *Dr.* Cash
>   *Cr.* Accounts receivable

This particular entry would probably be the first of many that he or she would make to record the day's business events in the furniture mart's journal for that day. The process of recording business transactions in this way is called **journalizing** the accounting entry.

Steps of the Accounting Process

Taking the various ideas discussed so far, we can summarize the steps in the accounting process as follows:

1. *Analysis of Transactions.* The first step in established accounting systems in organizations of some size is to assign an account number to a transaction in keeping with the organization's chart of accounts. A chart of accounts is a list of the various categories of expense and income used to accumulate the results of transactions for management control and for operating statements and balance sheets. Most charts of account use numbering systems that enable the organization to integrate responsibility reporting systems (in which expenses and, where appropriate, income are associated with a clearly defined organization unit) with financial reporting systems.

Charts of accounts prepared this way are as useful for periodic reports of performance against budget for the various expense and income categories of organizational units as they are for accumulation of profit center balance sheets and operating statements. For example, a chart of accounts may use an account number in the form 22.33.444, in which the first two numbers indicate the major organizational unit; the second two numbers, some significant separable activity of that unit, such as a smaller organizational unit, a special project, or a particular product; and the last three numbers, an expense category such as salaries, travel, and telephone and fax.

With these numbers as the basis, income and expenses can be summarized and totaled by major organization unit, by special project, by expense or income category, by reporting categories typically listed on balance sheets and operating statements, or by any of the many possible combinations of these approaches.

Every transaction must be understood and analyzed before it can be accounted for; thus, analysis is the first logical step in the accounting process. In this step, the accountant thinks through the effect of the transaction; that is, as cash increases and accounts receivable decrease, he or she translates these effects into specific debits and credits to the appropriate accounts—debit cash and credit accounts receivable.

2. *Journalization.* Journalization means the daily recording (in terms of debits and credits to the accounts) of each business transaction. The journal provides the accountant with his or her daily *record* of business events.

3. *Posting.* The third step in the accounting process is to transfer, or post, the information that has been recorded in the journal to all the accounts in the ledger.

4. *Adjusting.* Most business transactions take place as the result of an actual physical act that affects the business. Goods are sold, merchandise is delivered, cash payment is received, assets are purchased, and so on. Most accounting entries originate from such actual business transactions. In addition, however, the accountant needs to adjust the accounting of the business for other factors to present its financial situation accurately. Basically, this involves giving appropriate recognition to reduction in the value of the asset through its use or consumption in the business. Let's take the same two examples we used in exploring this concept in previous chapters.

Assume that the annual amount of the insurance premium of $1,200 was paid in advance. At the time this payment was made, the expenditure created an asset of prepaid insurance. As each month passes, the asset loses some of its value, since the period of coverage is constantly being reduced. On a twelve-month basis, the monthly reduction in value is $100. This fact needs to be reflected in the accounts, which is done by means of an "adjusting entry" that shows the reduction in the value of the asset and the increase in expense by means of the following entry in the journal:

Dr. Insurance expense $100
   Cr. Prepaid assets (insurance) $100

Depreciation is another basic entry that must be made in each accounting period to adjust the accounts of the business. We have discussed the process and rationale used to establish depreciation rates. However, the accountant can reflect these costs in the income statement and adjust the value of the fixed assets on the balance sheet only if he or she remembers to make the adjusting entries at the end of the accounting period.

Like other entries, adjusting entries are included in the journal. They are distinct from entries involving other transactions in that they are triggered only by the mental steps that the accountant takes accurately to adjust the accounts of the business.

5. *Closing.* Earlier we prepared an income statement for Gerry Manero by the simple procedure of subtracting the one or two expense transactions from the sum of revenue transactions. Under normal accounting procedure, the revenue and expense accounts of an income statement are actually "closed."

To understand the closing step, we must appreciate the fact that there are two types of accounts—real and temporary. Accounts for the income statement are temporary, whereas accounts for the balance sheet are real. This means that at the end of the accounting period, be it a month or a year, the so-called temporary accounts, or income statement accounts, are actually closed out. That is, they are balanced out so that the debit and credit sides are equal, thus making the new opening balance zero. Real accounts, or balance sheet accounts, are never closed. They always have a debit or a credit balance.

The closing process involves the steps that are used to take every account that appears on the income statement and close it (bring it to zero). The final net income account will then be closed to shareholders' equity account on the balance sheet. This is, of course, consistent with the concept that the shareholders' equity account increases with the net income for the accounting period. Later we illustrate the accountant's closing procedures with a step-by-step example.

6. *Preparation of Financial Statements.* The final step in the accounting process is preparation of financial statements. This in-

volves extracting information from accounts listed in the company's ledger and presenting it in accordance with a standard Balance Sheet and Income Statement format.

The Accounting Process Illustrated

Let's turn now to an application of these six steps in the accounting process, again using Gerry Manero's business as the example. In reviewing each transaction, we will start by going through the first three of the six steps required—analysis, journalization, and posting. Once this is done, we will continue to adjust and close the accounts and then prepare financial statements.

As a first step, we need to confirm the opening balances of our various accounts. To do this, we look first at Gerry Manero's balance sheet:

GERRY MANERO'S FURNITURE MART
Balance Sheet
December 31, 19X5

	Assets			*Equities*		
			Accounts payable	$ 100		
Cash	$ 300		Total current liabilities		$ 100
Accounts receivable	200		Notes payable		2,000
Inventories	3,600		Owner's equity		
Total current assets		$4,100	Capital stock	$5,000	
Fixed assets		5,000	Retained earnings	2,600	
Prepaid assets		600	Total owner's equity		7,600
Total assets		$9,700	Total equities		$9,700

The underlying ledger in support of this balance sheet appears in Exhibit 7-2, which shows that there is a ledger account for every item that appears on the balance sheet. Moreover, the balances in the ledger accounts correspond to the amounts shown on the balance sheet. Since balance sheet accounts are never closed, they always reflect a credit or debit balance unless there is nothing of value to be recorded in the account.

Exhibit 7-2. Basic general ledger for balance sheet accounts.

Assets		Equities	
Dr.	Cr.	Dr.	Cr.
+	−	−	+

Cash		Accounts Payable	
$300			$100

Accounts Receivable		Notes Payable	
$200			$2,000

Inventories		Capital Stock	
$3,600			$5,000

Fixed Assets		Retained Earnings	
$5,000			$2,600

Prepaid Assets	
$600	

We might note one further point. In the ledger, the account cash shows a balance of $300. We know that cash is an asset and that assets are increased with a debit and decreased with a credit. Since the converse is true for liabilities, we expect the values shown in these accounts to be reflected as credits on the right side of the account, as they are in Exhibit 7-2.

Exhibit 7-3 shows the so-called temporary or income statement accounts for the furniture mart. Note that none of these

Exhibit 7-3. Basic general ledger for income statement accounts.

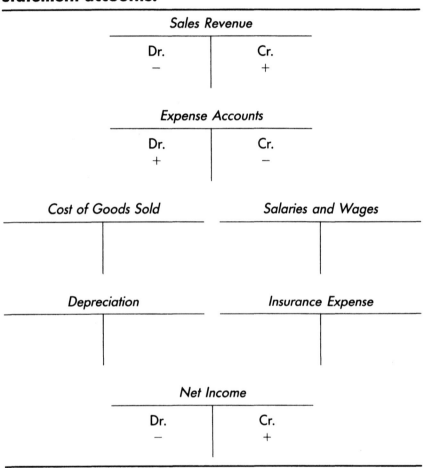

shows a balance, since they are temporary accounts and have a balance of zero from the closing of the last accounting period.

Now to our detailed application of the steps in the accounting process. Each transaction described has a corresponding entry in Exhibit 7-4, and transactions 6 and 7 appear in both Exhibit 7-4 and Exhibit 7-5.

Transaction 1. Customer pays $100 to the furniture mart, settling an outstanding accounts receivable.

Exhibit 7-4. Cumulative postings of balance sheet accounts.

Assets		Equities	
Dr.	Cr.	Dr.	Cr.
+	−	−	+

Cash		Accounts Payable	
$300*			$100*
†(1) $100	$100 (2)	(2) ($100)	
(3) 5,000	2,000 (4)		
(6) 3,000	1,000 (5)		
	600 (7)		

Accounts Receivable		Notes Payable	
$200*			$2,000*
	$100 (1)	(4) $2,000	

Inventories		Capital Stock	
$3,600*			$5,000*
(5) 1,000	$2,000 (6)		5,000 (3)

Fixed Assets		Retained Earnings	
$5,000*			$2,600*
	$50 adjusting entry		300

Prepaid Assets	
$600*	
	$50 adjusting entry

* Indicates opening balance
† Numbers in parentheses indicate transactions

Exhibit 7-5. Cumulative postings of income statement accounts.

Sales Revenue

Dr.	Cr.
–	+
	$3,000 (6)*

Expense Accounts

Dr.	Cr.
+	–

Cost of Goods Sold		Salaries and Wages	
*(6) $2,000		(7) $600	

Depreciation		Insurance Expense	
$50†		$50†	

Net Income

Dr.	Cr.
–	+

Key
* Numbers in parentheses indicate transactions.
† Adjusting entry.

Step 1, analysis of transaction. As a result of this transaction, the company has received $100 in cash. The asset cash increases by this amount, and the asset accounts receivable decreases by the same amount.

Step 2, journalization. The formal accounting treatment of this transaction in the journal is:

Dr. Cash $100
   Cr. Accounts receivable $100

Step 3, posting. The transaction would be posted to the T accounts in the ledger as follows:

Cash

Dr.	Cr.
+	–
$100	

Accounts Receivable

	$100

Transaction 2. The furniture mart pays $100 to a creditor, settling an account.

Step 1, analysis of transaction. The asset cash has been decreased by $100. At the same time a liability in the amount of $100, which was previously an account payable, has been reduced by the same amount.

Step 2, journalization.

Dr. Accounts payable $100
   Cr. Cash $100

Step 3, posting. The transaction is posted to the T accounts in the ledger as follows:

Cash		Accounts Payable	
Dr.	Cr.	Dr.	Cr.
+	–	–	+
	$100	$100	

Transaction 3. The furniture mart issues stock for a value of $5,000 to various members of the Manero family, receiving cash.

Step 1, analysis of transaction. The company has received $5,000 in cash, and the amount of this asset is increased by $5,000. At the same time, capital stock has been increased, since the sale of stock was the source of these funds. That equity increases by $5,000.

Step 2, journalization.

```
Dr. Cash . . . . . . . . . . . . . . . . . . . . . . . . $5,000
    Cr. Capital stock . . . . . . . . . . . . . . . . . .      $5,000
```

Step 3, posting. This transaction is posted to the T accounts in the ledger as follows:

Cash		Capital Stock	
Dr.	Cr.	Dr.	Cr.
+	−	−	+
$5,000			$5,000

Transaction 4. The furniture mart uses some of the proceeds it received from its stock issue to pay off its $2,000 note payable.

Step 1, analysis of transaction. The company has reduced its asset cash in the amount of $2,000. At the same time it has reduced a liability to a creditor, or a claim on its assets, by the same $2,000.

Step 2, journalization.

```
Dr. Notes payable . . . . . . . . . . . . . . . . . . . $2,000
    Cr. Cash . . . . . . . . . . . . . . . . . . . . . . .      $2,000
```

Step 3, posting. This transaction is posted to the T accounts of the ledger as follows:

Cash		Notes Payable	
Dr.	Cr.	Dr.	Cr.
+	−	−	+
	$2,000	$2,000	

Transaction 5. The company purchases merchandise for $1,000 in cash.

Step 1, analysis of transaction. The company has increased one of its assets, merchandise. At the same time, it has used another asset to make this purchase, cash, which has to be decreased.

Step 2, journalization.

Dr. Merchandise inventory $1,000
   Cr. Cash $1,000

Step 3, posting. This transaction is posted to the T accounts of the general ledger as follows:

Cash

Dr.	Cr.
+	−
	$1,000

Inventories

$1,000	

Transaction 6. The furniture mart sells merchandise that cost $2,000 for $3,000 cash.

Step 1, analysis of transaction. Several things have happened because of this transaction. It is the first event to affect the income statement, since the company has delivered merchandise and thereby obtained increased revenue. At the same time, because the merchandise was sold for cash, this asset is increased. In exchange, the furniture mart turns over merchandise that cost $2,000, decreasing the value of its inventory by this amount. This increases its expense, cost of goods sold, by the same amount.

Step 2, journalization. Journal entries for this transaction, because it involves several accounts, are four:

Dr. Cash $3,000
   Cr. Revenue (Exhibit 7-5) $3,000

Dr. Cost of goods sold (Exhibit 7-5) $2,000
   Cr. Merchandise Inventory (Exhibit 7-4) $2,000

Step 3, posting. This transaction is posted to the T accounts of the general ledger as follows:

BALANCE SHEET ACCOUNTS (Exhibit 7-4)

Cash

Dr.	Cr.
+	−
$3,000	

Inventories

+	$-$
	$2,000

INCOME STATEMENT ACCOUNTS (Exhibit 7-5)
Revenue

Dr.	Cr.
$-$	$+$
	$3,000

Cost of Goods Sold

Dr.	Cr.
$+$	$-$
$2,000	

Transaction 7. The furniture mart pays $600 of salaries and wages in cash.

Step 1, analysis of transaction. The asset cash decreases by $600; the expense salaries and wages increases by the same amount.

Step 2, journalization.

Dr. Expenses (salaries and wages; Exhibit 7-5) $600
  Cr. Cash (Exhibit 7-4) $600

Step 3, posting. This transaction is posted to the T accounts of the general ledger as follows:

BALANCE SHEET
Cash

Dr.	Cr.
$+$	$-$
	$600

INCOME STATEMENT
Salaries and Wages

Dr.	Cr.
$+$	$-$
$600	

For the preceding seven transactions, we have carried out the first three steps involved in the accounting process—analysis, journalization, and posting. We should again make clear that in our example the posting has been done at the same time as both of the other steps. However, in actual practice, the journal would probably be posted to the company's ledger as a separate step, later in the day or even at the end of the week or the month.

Adjusting

We noted earlier that at the end of each accounting period it is necessary to think through the adjustments that need to be made to reflect accurately the status of the business. Usually these adjustments involve recognition of expense that arises from the use of an asset during the accounting period under consideration.

In our case, there are fixed assets of $5,000 and prepaid assets of $600. The fixed asset consists of a Volkswagen delivery van for which we shall assume an annual depreciation cost of $600. Prepaid assets consist of a prepaid insurance premium.

If we assume, for the sake of simplicity, that the business transactions have spanned the period of a month, the values of both these assets need to be adjusted (with a corresponding expense increase) to reflect their usage during this period.

In the case of the Volkswagen, if the annual rate of depreciation is $600, then the monthly rate is $50. The accountant needs to reflect a decrease in the value of fixed assets of this amount and a corresponding increase in expense. We said earlier that rather than entering a direct deduction from the value of fixed assets, the accountant uses an allowance for depreciation. We, however, shall simply make the entry directly to fixed assets. The depreciation adjustment for the month of January 19X6 would result in the following journal entries:

Dr. Depreciation expense $50
    Cr. Fixed assets $50

The transaction would be posted to T accounts of the general ledger as follows:

BALANCE SHEET

Fixed Assets

Dr.	Cr.
+	−
	$50

INCOME STATEMENT

Depreciation Expenses

Dr.	Cr.
+	−
$50	

The prepaid asset consists of an annual insurance premium that has been paid in advance. Its value also decreases at a rate of $50 per month, with adjusting entries that would appear in journal form as follows:

```
Dr. Insurance expense . . . . . . . . . . . . . . . . . . $50
    Cr. Prepaid assets
        Insurance   . . . . . . . . . . . . . . . . . . . . . . $50
```

Posting to T accounts in the ledger, we have

BALANCE SHEET

Prepaid Assets

Dr.	Cr.
+	−
	$50

INCOME STATEMENT

Insurance Expense

Dr.	Cr.
+	−
$50	

Although we have listed the adjusting step as a separate phase of the accounting process, it also involves analysis as well as journalization of the appropriate accounting entries.

The Closing Process

We said earlier that the income statement accounts were temporary accounts that had to be closed at the end of each accounting period. This closing involves taking each account and establishing the debit or credit entry that is necessary to bring the account to a zero balance. The following step-by-step procedure illustrates this logical process.

Closing the Revenue Account

Exhibit 7-5 is the income statement of the furniture mart, with the entries of the transactions posted to each of the T accounts. The first account is revenue, which has a credit balance of $3,000. If we want this account to equal zero, or close it out, we must debit for $3,000. We want to close the revenue account to the net income account, so the other half of the entry will be a credit to net income:

Dr. Revenue $3,000
     Cr. Net income $3,000

Closing the Expense Accounts

The next step is to close the expense accounts to net income. The first of these is cost of goods sold, which has a debit balance of $2,000. To close it, we must make a credit entry of $2,000. That is, the balancing debit portion of the entry must be to net income for the same amount, thus:

```
Dr. Net income . . . . . . . . . . . . . . . . . . . $2,000
    Cr. Cost of goods sold . . . . . . . . . . . . . . . $2,000
```

The next expense account is salaries and wages, which has a debit balance of $600. To be closed, it must also have a credit entry of $600, thus:

```
Dr. Net income . . . . . . . . . . . . . . . . . . . $600
    Cr. Salaries and wages . . . . . . . . . . . . . . . $600
```

The depreciation and insurance accounts show a balance of $50 each. They receive exactly the same treatment as the other two expense accounts, and we have:

```
Dr. Net income . . . . . . . . . . . . . . . . . . . $50
    Cr. Depreciation expense . . . . . . . . . . . . . . $50

Dr. Net income . . . . . . . . . . . . . . . . . . . $50
    Cr. Insurance expense . . . . . . . . . . . . . . . $50
```

Closing the Net Income Account

All the accounts in the income statement have been closed except for the final one, net income. It, too, must be closed. By adding the debits and credits, we arrive at a debit balance of $2,700 and a credit balance of $3,000.

To close the account, we must make a debit entry of $300. The other half of the entry is to be a credit to owner's equity. In formal form:

```
Dr. Net income . . . . . . . . . . . . . . . . . . . $300
    Cr. Owner's equity (retained earnings, Exhibit 7-1) . . . . $300
```

Throughout the closing process, and particularly in this last step, we can see the consistent relationship between the mechanics of the accounting process and the basic accounting concepts. The credit to owner's equity in the closing of the net income account is, of course, an increase—which is exactly how we described the function of the income statement in conceptual terms.

GERRY MANERO'S FURNITURE MART
Balance Sheet
January 31, 19X6

Assets			Equities	
Cash	$4,700			
Accounts receivable	100		Accounts payable	0
Inventories	2,600		Notes payable	0
Current assets		$ 7,400	Owner's equity	
Fixed assets	$4,950		Capital stock	$10,000
Prepaid assets	550	5,500	Retained earnings	2,900
Total assets		$12,900	Total equities	$12,900

GERRY MANERO'S FURNITURE MART
Income Statement
For Period Ending January 31, 19X6

Sales revenue	$3,000
Less cost of goods sold	2,000
Gross margin	$1,000
Less	
Salaries and wages	600
Depreciation expense	50
Insurance expense	50
Total expenses	700
Net income	$ 300

Preparation of Financial Statements

The final step in the accounting process is the preparation of financial statements. To do this, we simply take the balances that appear in the ledger of accounts for the balance sheet and income statement and cast them into the conventional format for both these statements. Examples are shown for Gerry Manero's Furniture Mart.

We have worked with only a few very simple business transactions to account for Gerry Manero's efforts. The principles, procedures, and processes discussed in this chapter and employed in the last several illustrations, however, are exactly those that an accountant would use, no matter how numerous or complex the transactions. Stripped of its jargon, the basic accounting process is rather logical and simple.

8

Manufacturing and Merchandising Cost Essentials

So far we have dealt only with the concepts and procedures involved in accounting for business transactions that involve the purchase and resale of merchandise.

We should recognize that manufacturing cost accounting, or **cost accounting,** as it is usually called, is a subject unto itself and worthy of treatment in one, if not several, books. In this chapter we discuss only some fundamental concepts, particularly those that lead to a better understanding of the financial results of a manufacturing enterprise.

Merchandising vs. Manufacturing

Merchandising is a rather simple, straightforward process. It involves the purchase and ultimate resale of a product. Gerry Manero, like the local merchants with whom we all deal, is a merchandiser or merchant.

The manufacturer differs from the merchandiser in that he or she makes the product he or she sells. This involves either conversion or fabrication that starts with some form of a raw material that is subjected to a manufacturing process requiring either machinery or labor, probably both. Let us suppose that the EZI Manufacturing Company is involved with the manufacture of widgets. The firm has determined that it costs $10 to make a widget. This consists of:

- *Material:* $5 for the cost of the raw material.
- *Labor:* $3 for the cost of the labor for the time involved in making the widget.
- *Factory overhead:* $2 for the general costs of the factory in which the widget is manufactured. This includes heat, light, power, janitorial services, and similar expenses.

In most cases, accounting for the manufacturing costs of material and labor is not unduly difficult. Factory overhead is where the wicket, or if you will, the widget, gets a bit sticky. To see why this is so, let's look at Exhibit 8-1, which shows the categories of costs with which the accountant must work.

Of the five basic types of costs shown in Exhibit 8-1, the first three—labor, material, and factory overhead—are unique to the manufacturer. The last two, general and administrative expenses and selling expenses, are common to manufacturers and merchandisers. In manufacturing cost accounting, the problem arises because the difference between expenses that are factory overhead and those that are listed under general and administrative expenses is often fuzzy.

Assume, for example, that EZI Manufacturing Company has a large factory in which it manufactures widgets. The same building contains offices for the general manager, the accounting staff, the purchasing department, the engineering control group, and the sales department. Just one of the accountant's problems is to determine how all the costs associated with this building—taxes, insurance, heat and power, and so on—are to be divided between factory overhead and general and administrative expenses. This division of costs is by no means impossible, but since the costs are common to both categories, there are no correct scientific delineations. This is only one example, but once we appreciate the difficulty of precise identification of costs in each category, we can turn to the consequences of this problem.

Exhibit 8-1. Cost elements and their accounting treatment.

Cost Elements	Cost of Merchandiser	Cost of Manufacturer	Clear-Cut Product Costs	Clear-Cut Period Costs	Period and Product Cost	Accounting Treatment
Direct labor		X	X			Product
Direct material		X	X			Product
Factory overhead		X			X	Product — same division made as to product vs. period
General and administrative expense	X	X			X	Period
Selling expense	X	X		X		Period

Period vs. Product Expenses

Returning to Exhibit 8-1, we can see that five general categories of costs have been separated into two broad groups—product expenses and period expenses.

Product expenses, as the name suggests, are those costs that vary with each product made. Direct material is an excellent example. We have said that there is $5 of material in every widget; every time another widget is made, the expenses for the accounting period in which it was made increases $5. Labor is also generally considered to be a product cost. It may not always vary as directly with production as does material cost, but like material costs it can be directly identified with the manufacture of the product.

Period costs generally can be thought of as overhead costs. They consist, as the exhibit shows, of general and administrative expenses. Period costs derive their name from the fact that they occur over a period of time, regardless of the volume of goods produced or sold. For example, the property taxes on the factory in which the EZI Company manufactures widgets obviously do not increase with each additional widget that is manufactured. The same is true for insurance. Selling expenses, too, depend not on the number of units manufactured but on the sales effort. These indirect costs can be assigned only to a period of time by the accountant, usually on the basis of when they were incurred.

As Exhibit 8-1 illustrates, there is a gray area between the clear-cut period costs and product costs. That area includes many types of expenses that are not readily identifiable as one or the other. In reality, they are probably a bit of both. Despite this fact, in manufacturing accounting the accountant must make a delineation. It is even more important to understand that the manner in which this delineation is made (and it always must be made) can have a profound influence on the net income that is reported for the business.

Let's explore this proposition more specifically, recalling the accounting life cycle of converting assets to expenses. As an asset is consumed in the business, it becomes an expense. When goods are purchased, they become an asset—inventory. At the time of sale, when they are turned over to the customer, they become an expense—cost of goods sold.

The manufacturer also carries inventories; however, he or she makes rather than purchases his or her inventories. The values that he or she assigns to his or her inventories and cost of goods sold are what it has cost him or her to make the product. The costs to make a manufactured product are those of material, labor, and factory overhead.

We have seen, however, that in practice there is considerable imprecision in differentiating between factory overhead and general and administrative expenses. If the accountant decides that some of the expenses in the gray area between period costs and product costs are in fact product costs, then these costs are reflected as part of the value of the manufacturer's inventory. Thus, *they are shown as an asset rather than as an expense until the products are sold.* If, conversely, the accountant decides that the expense in question is a period expense, *it is shown as an expense for the accounting period rather than as an asset.*

To illustrate this phenomenon, let's look at XYZ Tool Machinery, Inc., and at the dramatically different financial results that company can obtain from the same manufacturing costs—depending on the decisions it makes regarding period versus product costs.

XYZ TOOL MACHINERY, INC.
Production for Period: Five Units (Machine Tools)
Sales for Period: Three Units (Machine Tools)

Costs to Produce and Sell Five Units

Labor	$250,000
Material	200,000
Overhead	
Factory General and administrative }	500,000
Selling	100,000

The distinction between factory overhead and general and

Exhibit 8-2. Calculation of inventory unit costs and general and administrative expenses.

	COST OF GOODS SOLD			
	Case A		Case B	
	Total	Per Unit	Total	Per Unit
Labor	$250,000	$ 50,000	$250,000	$ 50,000
Materials	200,000	40,000	200,000	40,000
Overhead				
80% × $500,000	400,000	80,000		
50% × $500,000			250,000	50,000
Totals	$850,000	$170,000	$700,000	$140,000

GENERAL AND ADMINISTRATIVE EXPENSES		
	Case A	Case B
Overhead		
Factory ⎫ General and ⎬ administrative ⎭	$500,000	$500,000
Designated as factory overhead	$400,000	$250,000
Balance, designated as general and administrative expense for the period	$100,000	$250,000

administrative expenses is unclear. In Case A (see Exhibit 8-2) the accountant assumes that 80 percent of overhead costs are product costs. In Case B she assumes that only 50 percent of the overhead costs are product costs. With these assumptions, the calculation of product costs for the cost of goods sold and inventories for the period is as shown in Exhibit 8-2.

The net income for the period, on the basis of the sales of three units of machine tools at a price of $250,000 per unit, would appear as in Exhibit 8-3.

Exhibit 8-3. Calculation of net income.

	Case A		Case B	
	Per Unit	Total	Per Unit	Total
Sales revenue (3 units)	$250,000	$750,000	$250,000	$750,000
Less cost of goods sold (3 units)	170,000	510,000	140,000	420,000
Gross margin	$ 80,000	$240,000	$110,000	$330,000
Selling expense		100,000		100,000
General and administrative expenses		100,000		250,000
Net income/loss before taxes		40,000		(20,000)
Value of inventory shown on balance sheet at end of accounting period (2 units)		$340,000		$280,000

We will leave unanswered the question as to whether the company made or lost money. In practice and with a great deal more information, accountants could undoubtedly arrive at a consensus. In fact, they do, since some choice must be made between period and product costs to determine the net income of a manufacturer. The convention of consistency, which requires that the same approach be used from one accounting period to another, can be of assistance in making manufacturing cost calculations more meaningful over an extended period. Still, the choice is less than scientific and can be significant. No one can make intelligent use of the accounting and financial data of a manufacturing organization without recognizing this fact.

Manufacturing Cost Systems

Basic as they may be, the concepts and issues we have discussed provide sufficient background for a brief and general discussion of different types of manufacturing cost systems: absorption cost systems, direct cost systems, standard cost systems, process cost systems, and activity-based costing.

Absorption Cost Systems

Another name for **absorption costing** is **full costing.** In this system, all three elements of manufacturing costs—direct labor, direct material, and factory overhead—are absorbed and charged to the product. In this manner, all the manufacturing costs are totally absorbed and figure as product expense, and none of them is taken as a period cost.

Absorption costing is the most conventional approach to manufacturing cost accounting, and the cost of goods sold that appears in the income statement of almost any major corporate manufacturing concern uses this method. The full absorption approach enables us to know that inventory values on the balance sheet include an element of factory overhead that will not be reflected as an expense in the income statement until the product is sold. In the preceding section, we discussed some of the difficulties and implications of defining factory overhead costs which must be assigned to the product under the absorption costing system.

Direct Cost Systems

Absorption cost accounting systems are used, and in fact are mandatory, for government as well as public financial reporting. The continuing emphasis on the use of accounting data for management purposes has brought into being an alternative method of manufacturing cost accounting, called **direct cost accounting.** This method is almost always used exclusively for internal purposes and is therefore employed in addition to absorption cost accounting.

In direct cost accounting only those elements that can be clearly and directly identified with the manufacture of each product are charged as the cost of that product, usually only direct material and labor. Thus the subtleties and vagaries of allocating overhead between products and periods are totally avoided.

The effect of direct versus absorption cost accounting is illustrated in Exhibit 8-4, which shows that under direct costing the elements of manufacturing overhead are charged not to the product but to the period in which they were incurred. When this approach is used, net income for the period more directly corresponds to the sales activity. This particular aspect of direct costing is one of its major attractions to its advocates, who argue that in fact it is much more accurate to have net income respond to sales. They further argue that the whole process of overhead determination and allocation to products is of necessity fuzzy and difficult. Therefore, nothing is really served by the whole process, since it tends to cloud rather than to clarify financial results.

Furthermore, the amount of overhead that gets charged under absorption costing depends on the physical volume of units that are manufactured. This figure can give a higher or lower cost per unit of manufacture but tends to be somewhat misleading, since the total amount of overhead costs will not have varied. For all these reasons, more and more businesses are using direct manufacturing cost accounting systems for internal managerial control and decision purposes.

Standard Cost Systems

Like those behind direct costing, the concepts of **standard costing** grew out of the continuing search for a more effective use of accounting data for managerial purposes. Throughout our discussion of manufacturing costs, we have been thinking in terms of costs as they were incurred and recorded in the accounting records of a manufacturing enterprise. This is historical cost data and tells management only what costs were. The idea behind standard costing, however, is to provide management with information as to what costs should be, rather than simply what they were.

By definition, "standard" implies a benchmark or a yardstick of performance. Since standard costs are meant to serve as a criterion for efficiency rather than simply to register what has actually happened, they must be well thought out and accurate. More often than not, they are engineered; that is to say, they are determined after a thorough and scientific investigation of what costs should be incurred to manufacture a product.

Exhibit 8-4. Direct versus absorption cost accounting.

	Accounting Period 1	Accounting Period 2
Production in units	5	5
Sales in units	3	7
Sales price per unit	$250,000	$250,000
Costs		
Labor		250,000
Material		200,000
Factory overhead*		250,000
General and administrative expenses		250,000
Selling		100,000

* Factory overhead and general and administrative expenses have been distributed as per Case B in Exhibit 8-3.

FACTORY OVERHEAD UNIT COST

Period	Total Factory Overhead Cost	Units Produced	Factory Overhead Per Unit
1	$250,000	5	$50,000
2	250,000	5	50,000

Unit Cost	Absorption	Direct
Labor	$ 50,000	$50,000
Material	40,000	40,000
Factory overhead	50,000	0
Totals	$140,000	$90,000

COSTS OF GOODS SOLD

Period	Sales Units	Absorption Costs Per Unit	Absorption Costs For Period	Direct Costs Per Unit	Direct Costs For Period
1	3	$140,000	$ 420,000	$90,000	$270,000
2	7	140,000	980,000	90,000	630,000
Totals	10		$1,400,000		$900,000

Exhibit 8-4. *(continued)*

	Absorption Costing		Direct Costing	
	Period 1	*Period 2*	*Period 1*	*Period 2*
Sales				
Units	3	7	3	7
Revenue	$750,000	$1,750,000	$750,000	$1,750,000
Less				
Labor	150,000	350,000	150,000	350,000
Material	120,000	280,000	120,000	280,000
Factory overhead	150,000	350,000	0	0
Cost of goods sold	420,000	980,000	270,000	630,000
Gross margin	$330,000	$ 770,000	$480,000	$1,120,000
Less				
Factory overhead	0	0	250,000	250,000
Selling expenses	100,000	100,000	100,000	100,000
General and administrative expenses	250,000	250,000	250,000	250,000
Total expenses	$350,000	$ 350,000	$600,000	$ 600,000
Net income/(loss)	(20,000)	420,000	(120,000)	520,000
Cumulative net income	$400,000		$400,000	
Ending inventory				
Units	2	0	2	0
Value	$280,000	0	$180,000	0

In the EZI Company's manufacture of widgets, for example, a standard costing system would be developed in conjunction with engineers who would, after analysis and time and motion studies, determine that a certain amount of money should be spent for raw materials for each product and a certain amount of overhead be incurred. These three elements in total would represent what should happen if the product is to be manufactured under efficient, well-managed conditions. Once this system is determined, all that is required is to record the total physical number

Exhibit 8-5. Income statement of XYZ Tool Machinery, Inc., under a standard costing system.

Sales	$2,500,000
Less	
Cost of goods sold at standard rate	$1,400,000
Variances	200,000
Cost of goods sold	$1,600,000
Gross profit	$ 900,000
Less	
Selling expenses	200,000
General and administrative expenses	500,000
Total Expenses	$ 700,000
Net income before taxes	$ 200,000
Variances	
Material variance (higher cost)	$ 100,000
Labor variance (higher cost)	100,000

of units manufactured during a given period and then to apply the standard cost rate to this volume of production. The result is the total shown as the standard cost of manufacture. Sometimes standard costs are built up on the basis of past experience and cost data, rather than predetermined through engineering studies.

Under a standard costing system, the procedures involved in the recording of actual costs are not discontinued. Actual costs incurred are also accounted for. They can then be compared against the standard costs, and the difference can be shown as a variance. A variance can be either favorable or unfavorable. If actual costs are less than those established in the standard costing system, the variance is favorable; if actual costs are higher, the variance is unfavorable. Exhibit 8-5 shows how the net income for XYZ Tool Machinery, Inc., might be recorded under a standard costing system.

The appeal of the standard costing system is obvious. It facilitates management's evaluation as to whether the manufacturing process is being carried on efficiently. By providing a continuing gauge of efficiency, it allows management to take action when necessary to correct a problem or inefficiency more quickly. Also, use of the system can often actually facilitate and simplify the accounting process. This is particularly true in the manufacture of high-volume items, where it becomes extremely difficult to record on an actual basis the cost of manufacture for each unit. It is important to recognize, however, that the final net income must always be based on the actual costs incurred and not on the standard cost. A standard costing system can involve standards only for direct costs and/or direct plus full costs. In other words, a standard costing system can be a direct standard costing system or a standard absorption costing system.

Process Cost Systems

The system of costing in which products are manufactured in a series of continuous processes and costs are accumulated by department or cost center is known as **process costing.** Process costing determines how manufacturing costs that are incurred during each period are to be allocated; the ultimate goal is to compute the total units costs for determining income. To accomplish this objective, individual work-in-process accounts are maintained for each production department or manufacturing process.

These work-in-process accounts accumulate direct material costs, direct labor costs, and factory overhead costs as the different processes are performed within each department. As units are completed in one department, they are transferred with their respective costs to another department. The next department receives the completed unit(s) from the previous department and considers the unit(s) a unit of raw material until all the processes are completed, at which time the units are considered a finished good.

A unit cost of production is calculated for each process, and the total cost of production represents the sum of the unit costs for each process through which a product must flow. To determine the unit cost of the process, the following simple calculation is made:

$$\frac{\text{Total cost in process}}{\text{Units produced in process}} = \begin{array}{l} \text{unit cost} \\ \text{of process} \end{array}$$

Products can flow through a factory toward completion in many ways. While the same costing system applies, they commonly follow one of three product flows: a sequential product flow, a parallel product flow, and a selective product flow.

1. *Sequential product flow.* **Sequential product flow** traces the movement of raw materials from one department to another until they are considered part of the finished goods inventory. All products follow the same processes in the same sequence, as illustrated.

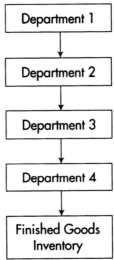

2. *Parallel product flow.* In **parallel product flow,** the initial materials are added during different processes that begin in different departments and are combined in the final process.

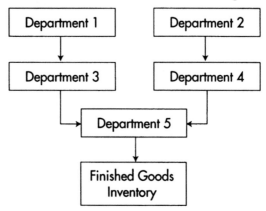

3. *Selective product flow.* In **selective product flow,** several products are produced from the same initial raw material.

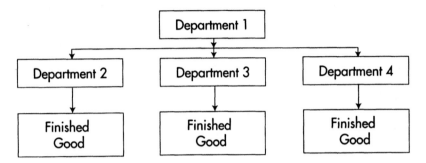

It is important to compute how many actual units have been produced without regard to the work performed. This is done by adding units started or transferred into production during the process period. The result is referred to as the **total units accounted for.** A sample calculation is presented in Exhibit 8-6.

Once the physical units are calculated, a measurement must be made of the productivity of each department. This is done by expressing physical units of output in terms of fully completed units. This is done by multiplying the percentage of work done by the physical units of output. For example, if Department A has a period output of 2,000 units and these units are only 50%

Exhibit 8-6. Calculating total units accounted for.

	Department A	Department B
Work-in-progress—beginning of month	1,000	200**
Started (transferred) into production	5,000	4,000
Total units to be accounted for	6,000	4,200
Transferred to Department B	4,000	3,500***
Work-in-process—end of month	1,000*	500****
Total units accounted for	5,000	4,000

* 40% complete
** 30% complete
*** Transferred to finished goods
**** 80% complete

complete, the equivalent units of production are 1,000 units (2,000 units × .50).

All costs are accumulated at the end of a period and summarized in a production cost report that shows both production quantity and cost data for each production department. This report contains five major categories of data: 1) units that are charged to each department, 2) units accounted for, 3) unit costs, 4) costs charged to each department, and 5) costs accounted for.

Activity-Based Costing (ABC)

Activity-based costing (ABC) is a costing system that uses activities as the fundamental method of costing to produce a product. The costs that are incurred are accumulated by activity and then transferred from the activities to the products produced, based on how much consumption was used by each activity for each product manufactured. The activity costs are then transferred to products as they move through the production process.

In today's environment, managers manage and focus on activities; if activities are managed effectively, a company experiences lower unit costs and becomes more competitive. A key element of using ABC is the allocation of activity costs by using cost drivers, which represent factors that result in changes in the total cost of a product. Through this method of costing, multiplied costing allocations produce more accurate cost calculations and lead to better decisions.

To use the ABC system, three elements must be identified: activities, the cost of those activities, and the primary cost drivers applied to each activity. The following is an example of an activity and its cost driver, or the basis of allocation.

Activity	Cost Driver
Purchasing of parts	Number of parts purchased
Raw material purchases	Number of orders placed
Storing of raw materials	Number of requisitions
Machine set-ups	Number of set-up hours
Financial reporting	Number of financial reports
Advertising	Number of specific media placements

To illustrate how a product is costed using the ABC method, let us assume the following facts.

The production of Product X requires six activities as follows:

1. Ordering raw materials
2. Receiving raw materials
3. Warehousing raw materials
4. Transporting raw materials to assembly area
5. Assembling raw materials
6. Inspecting finished units

Each of these activities has a cost and a cost driver that results in a per-unit conversion cost as follows:

Activity	Cost of Activity	Cost Driver	=	Conversion Cost
1	$ 100	Number of times ordered (40)		$2.50
2	250	Number of shipments (80)		3.13
3	300	Number of requisitions (100)		3.00
4	600	Number of times ordered (250)		2.40
5	1,500	Number of parts (300)		5.00
6	600	Number of finished units (100)		6.00

The manufacturing cost of Product X is computed as follows:

Direct materials	$7.85
Conversion costs:	
Order raw materials (2 orders × $2.50)	5.00
Receive raw materials (2 orders × $3.13)	6.26
Warehousing raw materials (3 req. × $3.00)	9.00
Transporting raw materials (2 orders × $2.40)	4.80
Assembling raw materials (3 parts × $5.00)	15.00
Inspecting finished units (2 units × $6.00)	12.00
Total manufacturing cost per unit	$59.91

In addition to these unit costs, other costs, such as those for marketing and distribution, must be added to the per unit cost of $59.91.

In summary, ABC costing, which uses more than one allocation base, provides management with more accurate costs than traditional cost systems, which have a single cost application base.

9

Other Basic Cost Concepts and Their Applications

In Chapter 8, we examined some of the concepts and issues involved in determining period versus product costs and then briefly discussed five basic types of primarily manufacturing cost accounting systems.

In this chapter, we explore various additional cost concepts and their application in the presentation and interpretation of management-oriented financial reports. We begin with a discussion of types of costs and their behavior.

Types of Costs

Costs are characterized in terms of their response to levels of activity.

Variable Costs

Costs that vary with each unit of activity are called, not surprisingly, **variable costs.** Raw material is perhaps the best illustration of a variable cost; with each unit manufactured, raw-materials cost varies directly. If 20 percent more units are manufactured, then raw materials costs (assuming there has been no increase in the cost of the raw material) will increase by 20 percent.

Semivariable Costs

Some costs vary with the amount of an activity, but not in a direct relationship to it. Such costs are called **semivariable costs;** they are "almost" variable. Semivariable costs differ from variable costs in that they do not vary directly with each unit of activity.

Maintenance costs are a common example of semivariable costs. For most machinery, there is a minimum maintenance cost that is independent of how much the machinery is used and, in addition, a maintenance expense that varies with machine usage. For example, most machines with moving parts that operate 96 hours per week need more maintenance than those that operate 16 hours, but probably only four times as much rather than six. The cost varies with the activity, but not in a direct relationship.

Fixed Costs

As the name suggests, **fixed costs** remain the same regardless of the level of activity or the number of units produced. A plant's property taxes and the depreciation expense on its equipment are typical examples of fixed costs.

Fixed costs, like almost any other in today's inflationary world, can, of course, increase. They are not fixed in the sense that they never increase or decrease; they simply do not increase or decrease in relation to the level of activity, as do the variable and semivariable costs we have already described.

The Total Cost Matrix

The total cost of any activities or organizations is made up of either variable, semivariable, or fixed costs—usually, a combination of all three. Exhibit 9-1 illustrates how the cost categories we have discussed normally respond to the basic expenses incurred by any business enterprise.

For a more specific, initial, and rather simplified illustration of these ideas, let's again draw upon the business endeavors of our old friend from Chapter 1, Gerry Manero. In this instance, we will assume that Gerry has sold his furniture mart and has gone into the business of manufacturing and selling widgets.

Exhibit 9-1. Cost categories as determined by sales and manufacturing activities.

Cost Description	Fixed	Semi-Variable	Varies With	Variable	Varies With
Building Rent	X				
Depreciation	X				
Raw Material				X	Units Manufactured
Wages for Labor	X*				
Management Salaries	X				
Packaging Material				X	Units Packaged
Maintenance		X	Units Manufactured		
Sales Commissions				X	Units Sold

*Wages would be variable if they were paid on a piece-rate basis, as is the case in some companies.

Here is some information concerning the results of Gerry's new business at the end of the first year of operation.

- Gerry manufactured his widgets in a small building that he rented for $300 a month, or $3,600 for the year. All utilities were included.
- At the outset of his venture, Gerry purchased a widget-molding machine at $12,000 installed. The estimated useful life is 10 years. On a straight-line basis (equal amounts each of the 10 years), the annual depreciation charge is $1,200.
- The cost of raw materials for each widget is $10.
- The cost of packaging material for each widget is $1.
- Gerry paid one attendant to run the widget-forming machine. His weekly wages and benefits amounted to $200.
- Gerry entered into a sales contract with a distributor who charged a sales commission of 10% of the selling price of each widget sold.
- During the first year of operation, 6,000 widgets were sold at a price of $20 per unit.

- Gerry paid himself a salary of $1,000 per month to manage his new business.
- At full capacity, four widgets per hour were manufactured. During a 40-hour week, 160 were produced.
- The widget machine that Gerry had purchased required cleaning and overhauling after every 100 hours of operation or every month, whichever occurred first. The manufacturer provided this service at a flat cost of $200 per overhaul.

Let's now take the concepts of fixed, variable, and semivariable costs and illustrate how they can be used to translate the foregoing list of Gerry's business activities into an informative management-oriented annual income statement as shown in Exhibit 9-2.

Other Cost Concepts

Now let's briefly look at some additional cost concepts and the terminology used to describe them.

Direct Costs

The term **direct cost** is often used synonymously with **variable cost** as it has been defined earlier in this section.

The cost of material varies directly with each unit manufactured; a variable cost, it is also a direct cost because it can be directly and specifically identified with the particular unit manufactured. In this instance, and any other, a variable cost is a direct cost. The variability of the cost, however, is not the factor that distinguishes it as a direct cost. Rather, the critical distinction lies in the cost's direct association with the particular unit involved.

Direct costs in this context can also be semivariable or fixed. They are referred to as direct costs because they can be directly identified with a given activity or responsibility center.

Advertising, for example, is not a variable cost, but it can be considered a direct cost and presented as such in assessing the profitability of a product line. The same is true for the costs of

Exhibit 9-2. Gerry's Widgets profit and loss statement for first year of operation.

Revenues

Annual sales of 6,000 widgets at $20 per unit	$120,000

Variable Expenses

Raw material—$10 per unit times 6,000 units manufactured	60,000	
Packaging material—$1 per unit times 6,000 units manufactured and packaged	6,000	
Sales commissions—10% commission per unit at selling price of $20 equals $2 per unit times 6,000 units	12,000	
Subtotal—Variable costs	$78,000	

Semivariable Expenses

Maintenance expense	$ 3,000	
6,000 units manufactured at capacity of 4 units per hour required 1,500 hours of machine operation; maintenance was required every 100 hours of operation, so 15 overhauls were required at $200 per overhaul, resulting in a total annual cost of $3,000		
Subtotal—Semivariable costs	$ 3,000	

Fixed Costs

Rent	$ 3,600	
Depreciation	1,200	
Labor—Annual wages for machine attendant	10,400	
Administration—Gerry's salary	12,000	
Subtotal—Fixed Costs	$27,200	
Total—All costs		$108,200
Net income before taxes (Revenues minus total costs)		$ 11,800

brand management and market research associated with the support of that product.

More often than not, maintenance is a semivariable expense—but if that maintenance cost is incurred exclusively on machines that manufacture a product, it is considered a direct cost for that particular product. The concept of direct costs can also be explained by contrasting them with indirect costs.

Indirect Costs

As the term implies, **indirect costs** cannot be identified with any particular activity or product. Typical examples of indirect costs are the expenses associated with the corporate president's office, the corporate secretary's office, and the corporate controller's department. Although the costs of these functions and activities are critical to the overall conduct of company business, it is usually difficult to associate any one of them directly with a particular product or particular segment of the company. Since they can't be directly associated with any specific activity, they are often "allocated." To allocate means to *place* or to *apportion*—and usually this is just what happens. Indirect costs are apportioned to products, branches, factories, divisions, or other company elements on one basis or another. The bases or combination of bases for these allocations are numerous. While there is no "correct" base, here are some of the more common ones:

- The sales total of a product or division in relation to total company sales
- The direct costs of a product or division in relation to the total direct costs of all company products and/or divisions
- The assets related to a product or division in relation to total company assets
- The number of employees in a division in relation to the total number of employees in the company

All these methods rely on a set formula for allocation. Often, however, indirect costs are based upon "time or effort" allocations. Under this system, the group generating the indirect costs estimates (or sometimes actually records) the time and effort it devotes to its particular segment of the company. Thus, the corporate legal counsel many indicate that he or she devotes 60 percent of his or her time to the consumer products division, 25 percent to the industrial products division, and 15 percent to the specialty products division. Each division is charged accordingly.

Later in this chapter, we analyze more thoroughly the relevance of indirect costs in various business decisions. Our purpose at the moment is to acquaint you with these concepts, for they have come to play an increasing role in the design of various internal and sometimes external financial reports. A typical example of their application might look like the report shown in Exhibit 9-3.

The Contribution Concept

The **contribution concept** is at the heart of business decisions based on cost considerations. In essence, the contribution method sorts out costs in terms of their behavior (fixed, semivariable, or variable) and their nature (direct or indirect) in order to arrive at intelligent business decisions concerning such questions as the following:

- Should a certain sales territory be closed?
- Should another sales territory be expanded?
- Should a certain product be dropped?
- Should a certain special sales order be taken?

Let's return to Gerry's widget business to take a closer look at some of these ideas. If you refer to the profit and loss statement for Gerry's Widgets in Exhibit 9-2, you will recall that he was selling his widgets at $20 each. Let's now suppose that he has an offer to sell an additional thousand, but at a price of $15. The obvious question is, should he?

From his profit and loss statement, we know that Gerry expects to incur annual costs of $108,200 to manufacture and sell 6,000 widgets. For the sake of simplicity, we assume that all these

Exhibit 9-3. Sample application of direct and indirect costs.

	Consumer Division	Industrial Division	Specialty Division
Sales	$500,000	$350,000	$100,000
Less Direct variable and semivariable manufacturing costs	310,000	200,000	40,000
Subtotal	190,000	150,000	60,000
Less Direct fixed manufacturing costs	40,000	50,000	20,000
Gross Margin	150,000	100,000	40,000
Less Direct selling expenses	50,000	18,000	12,000
Direct administrative expenses	25,000	10,000	5,000
Total Direct S & A Expenses	75,000	28,000	17,000
Subtotal—Division Contribution	75,000	72,000	23,000
Less Indirect selling expenses	20,000	25,000	2,000
Indirect administrative expenses	5,000	10,000	1,000
Total Indirect S & A Expenses	25,000	35,000	3,000
Subtotal—Division income before tax and interest	$ 50,000	$ 37,000	$ 20,000

costs are associated with the manufacture of widgets (that is, they are all product costs). Therefore, the cost per widget under the absorption cost concept would be:

$$\frac{\text{Costs}}{\text{Widgets}} = \frac{\$108,200}{6,000} = \$18.03 \text{ per widget}$$

If each widget costs $18.03 to manufacture but can be sold under special order at only $15, it certainly seems that Gerry should decline the order. This rather superficial but nonetheless conventional analysis ignores the various types of cost behavior and could lead Gerry to the wrong decision. While it's true that

Exhibit 9-4. Contribution analysis of the per-unit profitability of Gerry's special widget order.

Revenue per Unit		$15.00
Less		
Variable and semivariable unit costs		
Raw material	$10.00	
Packaging material	1.00	
Sales commission—10% on $15 per widget	1.50	
Maintenance expense	.50	
Total variable and semivariable costs		13.00
Unit contribution to fixed expenses and profit		$ 2.00

Note: These figures are taken from Gerry's annual income statement, shown in Exhibit 9-2. Maintenance expense is calculated as follows: cost per overhaul ($200) divided by hours of operation requiring overhaul (100) equals an average maintenance expense of $2 per hour. Since 4 units are produced per hour, $2 divided by 4 yields a per-unit maintenance cost of 50 cents.

Gerry's total costs are $108,200 to make 6,000 widgets, we know that $27,200 of these are fixed and $3,000 are semivariable. The calculation of a total cost of $18.03 per unit and the use of this figure in making this decision assumes that all costs are variable—which is, of course, not true for Gerry's business or any other.

Under the contribution concept, Gerry's proposal would be analyzed in terms of exactly what costs would vary with (or be directly associated with) the decision to manufacture and sell 1,000 widgets at a price of $15 per widget. Exhibit 9-4 illustrates the contribution approach to the analysis of this proposal.

When the proposal is analyzed as we have shown, it becomes clear that instead of losing money, Gerry would actually end up with a contribution to fixed expenses and a net income of $2 per unit. Based on the order of 1,000 widgets, his profits would increase $2,000 compared to profits if he were to decline the order. The reason, of course, is that his fixed costs would not increase as a result of the new business. Thus, the contribution would actually be a straight contribution or increase in net income; thus, it appears that Gerry should take the order.

For Gerry or any other businessperson in a similar situation, there is an additional critical consideration. This is supposedly a special order—but before Gerry fills it, he needs to consider whether his other customers might request widgets at a price of $15 rather than $20. Should this be the case, this one decision that makes sense over the short term could spell disaster for the business over the long term.

Variable or direct costs are also often referred to as **marginal costs** and contribution as **marginal income.** Direct costing and contribution analysis have been among the most significant developments in management accounting techniques. But this tool, like any other, cannot be used blindly. There's an old saying that many businesses have gone to their grave "dancing to the magic music of marginal costs."

Other Applications
of the Contribution Concept

The simplicity of Gerry's widget business facilitates an explanation of the contribution concept, but the basic idea remains the same however complex the problem or organization. Let's look at some applications in situations more likely to be encountered by the successful manager in a larger business organization, EZ Corporation.

Assume, for example, that management wants to review the profitability of various sales territories and is presented with the conventional information for this purpose (see Exhibit 9-5). Looking at this information, management is likely to conclude that region C is unprofitable and region B marginal.

Under the contribution concept, the same information would be presented as it appears in Exhibit 9-6. The similarity to Gerry's special widget order is obvious, an analysis based on the contribution concept changes our perception of the comparative profitability of the sales region. Even though the problem is different, the basic approach is the same—namely, to identify specific cost behavior and determine the directness of its association with the

Exhibit 9-5. Analysis of sales region profitability.

EZ CORPORATION

	Region A	Region B	Region C	Total
Sales	$500,000	$300,000	$200,000	$1,000,000
Less				
Cost of goods sold[1]	300,000	200,000	150,000	650,000
Gross margin	200,000	100,000	50,000	350,000
Less				
Transportation expenses	25,000	30,000	15,000	70,000
Sales commissions	40,000	25,000	10,000	75,000
Selling expenses[2]	60,000	20,000	30,000	110,000
Admn. expenses[2]	30,000	20,000	10,000	60,000
Expense subtotal	155,000	95,000	65,000	315,000
Operating profit/(loss)	$ 45,000	$ 5,000	($ 15,000)	$ 35,000

[1] All goods produced at central manufacturing location. Figures include head office allocations of indirect manufacturing fixed overhead.
[2] Include head office allocations of indirect fixed expenses as follows:

	Region A	Region B	Region C	Total
Selling	$15,000	$15,000	$15,000	$45,000
Administrative	5,000	5,000	5,000	15,000
Total	$20,000	$20,000	$20,000	$60,000

activity (or decision) being analyzed. In the case of EZ Corporation, all the regions make a sizeable contribution to indirect fixed expenses. But how about region C, which shows a loss in the analysis in Exhibit 9-5? If management decides on that basis to close it, contribution analysis shows that—even with the region's direct fixed costs eliminated—there will be a reduction of $80,000 in contribution to indirect corporate fixed costs (which will not, of course, be reduced), and the corporation will be thrown into a loss.

Finally, Exhibit 9-7 presents a typical illustration of how an assessment of product profitability might be made under the contribution concept. Obviously, the essence of the contribution concept involves identifying costs by their behavior pattern. Under

Exhibit 9-6. Contribution analysis by sales region.

EZ CORPORATION

	Region A	Region B	Region C	Total
Sales	$500,000	$300,000	$200,000	$1,000,000
Less				
Variable costs				
Production	250,000	160,000	75,000	485,000
Marketing				
Transportation	25,000	30,000	15,000	70,000
Commissions	40,000	25,000	10,000	75,000
Total variable costs	315,000	215,000	100,000	630,000
Contribution after				
variable costs	185,000	85,000	100,000	370,000
Less				
Direct fixed costs[1]				
Selling	45,000	5,000	15,000	65,000
Administrative	25,000	15,000	5,000	45,000
Total direct fixed costs	70,000	20,000	20,000	110,000
Region contribution	$115,000	$ 65,000	$ 80,000	$ 260,000
Less				
Indirect fixed expenses				
Manufacturing				165,000
Selling				45,000
Administrative				15,000
Total indirect fixed expenses				225,000
Operating profit				$ 35,000

[1] Direct fixed costs by region were obtained by deducting allocations of fixed selling and administrative expenses in Note 2, Table 9.5.

contribution analysis, costs relevant to the decision at hand are analyzed to determine whether—and by how much—that cost will vary as a result of the decision.

With Gerry's special widget order, contribution analysis facilitated an assessment of the economic consequences of the decision he had to make. This was also true for the EZ Corporation's analysis of profitability by sales region.

Exhibit 9-7. Analysis of contribution by product.

EZ CORPORATION

	Product X	Product Y	Product Z	Total
Sales	$230,000	$125,000	$42,000	$397,000
Less Variable costs				
Production	125,000	70,000	20,000	215,000
Marketing— commissions	15,000	6,000	2,000	23,000
Marketing— transportation	7,000	2,400	500	9,900
Total variable costs	147,000	78,400	22,500	247,900
Contribution after variable costs	83,000	46,600	19,500	149,100
Less Direct fixed costs				
Production	0	0	0	0
Marketing	10,000	8,000	3,000	21,000
Total direct fixed costs	10,000	8,000	3,000	21,000
Product contribution	$ 73,000	$ 38,600	$16,500	$128,100
Less Indirect fixed expenses				
Manufacturing				40,000
Selling				20,000
Administrative				10,000
Total indirect fixed expenses				70,000
Operating profit				$ 58,100

For the manager, contribution analysis holds an additional attraction. From our exhibits, we can see that under the contribution concept a manager is never charged with an expense that his decision did not influence.

Compare, for example, the performance reading on sales region C in Exhibit 9-5 with that of the same region in Exhibit 9-6. In Exhibit 9-5, the performance of region C's manager was assessed after he had been charged with $20,000 of indirect selling and administrative expenses and $75,000 of indirect manufacturing fixed overhead. But these costs result from headquarters' decisions and actions, not his. Exhibit 9-6, which analyzes performance under the contribution concept, more accurately portrays his responsibility.

Controversy still surrounds the contribution (or direct cost) concept, and books continue to be written in praise or criticism of the technique. Even so, the acceptance and application of the contribution concept continues to grow. It is an essential part of any discussion or utilization of modern financial analysis.

10

Fundamentals of Investment Analysis: Evaluating New Investments—Some Basic Considerations

Twenty centuries ago Aristotle pointed out that the "first step is what counts." To end well, one must begin well. This notion is nowhere more true than in the evaluation of new investments. The success or failure of a new investment is largely determined by the accuracy with which it is initially assessed. For those investments that have tangible incentives, i.e., either savings or incremental earning, that assessment is whether the investment is justified by the earnings or savings it will create over its life.

In more common vernacular, we ask, what is the return on investment (ROI), and is it satisfactory?

In this and the next four chapters, we explore the tools and techniques that are used by management to quantify and evaluate the answer to this question.

First, by way of a bit of historical background, we should understand that the basic concept underlying return on investment—that capital is entitled to a return for its use—is almost as old as the use of money itself. In classical Greece, wealthy individuals loaned money to others for a return, and "money changers" were a familiar sight in biblical times.

Throughout the centuries, society has recognized that people are entitled to a return for the wise use of their money. In the early 1800s the English economist David Ricardo used this concept in his systematization of economics, laying the groundwork for modern economic systems. Ricardo defined the three basic factors of production as land, labor, and capital. Each element, said Ricardo, is entitled to a return for its use: the return on land for its contribution to the economic process is **rent;** the return on labor is **wages;** and the return on capital is **interest.**

This centuries-old concept is the backbone of our so-called modern technique. And just as the basic concept underlying return on investment is not truly modern, neither is it complex. A good way to demonstrate the basic simplicity of the ROI concept is to use an example familiar to all of us—the bank loan.

When a bank makes a loan, it is entitled, according to economic theory, to a return on its capital—its investment. This return is the interest you pay on the loan.

Let's assume you borrow $1,000 from your local bank at 8% interest. You agree to pay back the loan plus interest in five annual installments of $250 each. Your annual $250 payment includes a repayment of the bank's investment, or principal, and the interest—a return to the bank for the use of its money during the year. When the bank receives your payment each year, it deducts the interest charges; the remainder of the payment is used to repay the principal.

Exhibit 10-1 shows how each annual payment is divided into repayment of principal and of interest. At the end of the first year, the bank calculates the amount of interest due at 8%—a total of $80. When this amount is deducted from your first $250 annual payment, $170 remains to reduce the original investment, so at the end of the first year the balance outstanding on the principal of the loan is $830.

At the end of the second year, you make another payment of $250. Once again the bank deducts its return on investment and applies the balance of the payment ($184) to reducing the principal. The same procedure is followed for the remaining three payments. Finally, by the end of the fifth year, you will have repaid the amount of the loan and your banker will have received

Exhibit 10-1. Five annual payments of $250 on investment of $1,000.

Year	Annual Payment	Return of 8% on Investment at End of Year	Repayment of Principal	Bank's Investment at End of Year
0	—	—	—	$1,000
1	$250	$80	$170	830
2	250	66	184	646
3	250	52	198	448
4	250	36	214	234
5	250	19	231	3

a return of 8% on the principal outstanding at the end of each of the five years.

It is evident from this example that return is nothing more than the income that lenders or investors receive on funds they have either loaned or invested.

Even though the basic concept of return on investment is an old and simple one, its importance to modern business has never been greater. The chief executive of a highly capital-intensive company recognized the importance of ROI when he remarked: "Everyone recognizes that the name of the game is changing, and that the rules of the game are changing. But the fact that the scoring of the game must also change hasn't dawned on many people yet." By "scoring" he meant the way we measure a company's success. We have traditionally used earnings per share for this measure, but return on investment is now more relevant and timely.

William Hawlett, president of Consolidated Foods, has suggested pretty much the same thing. He suggested that we think of profit not in the conventional sense of net income but as an acronym for the phrase "*Proper Return On Funds Invested Today.*"

The basic concept of return on investment is neither new nor unduly complex. We should, however, explore further the basic steps and some of the nuances involved in the process of an ROI evaluation of new investments.

Keep in mind that the question of whether an investment is justified by the earnings or savings it will create over its life cannot be answered for all investments. Some investments do not have tangible incentives—such as savings or earnings—that can justify them. The construction of an employees' lunchroom or a waste-treatment facility may be one of the most important investments a business makes for its future, but the benefits of either of these investments cannot always be quantified. For investments of this kind, we have to rephrase our question: Is the investment justified by the *anticipated* benefits it will create over its life?

More frequently, however, the benefits associated with a particular investment are tangible and can be measured reasonably accurately. For these investments, as we pointed out earlier, the first consideration is whether the investment can be economically justified.

Let's look first at the almost self-evident basic steps involved in any financial, economic analysis of a new investment.

1. Identify and quantify the amount of the investment.
2. Determine the net savings and/or the earnings that will result from the investment.
3. Identify the effects of tax costs on the new savings or earnings that you expect from the investment. In some cases, tax consequences can also affect the amount of the investments, as in the case of investment credits and/or other such incentives.
4. Determine whether the investment is justified by the savings or earnings or by some of the intangible benefits it will create.

In principle, the basic steps in the investment process appear simple; in actual application, however, they can often become more complex. For example, we've said that the first step in any analysis of an investment is to identify the amount of the investment itself. What could be more simple? All we need to know is the cost of the machinery or equipment (and the costs involved in delivery and installation) in which we want to invest.

In practice, the problem of accurately assessing the real magnitude of any new investment is not always completely straightforward. For instance, is the investment in a new petroleum refinery only the cost of the refinery itself? What about the service stations that may need to be built to sell the gasoline? Or the trucks, the pipelines, and the tankers to transport the crude oil? This example illustrates an important point: you can't determine whether savings or earnings will justify an investment until you're sure how much that investment will be.

The second step in investment analysis calls for a determination of the net savings, earnings, or benefits. Here again, the seeming simplicity of the step belies the possible hazards involved. Why? Because, of necessity, estimates of savings or earnings must be based on assumptions about the behavior of costs or revenues in the future. And, as the old saying goes, "Forecasting is difficult when it pertains to the future."

Earnings estimates based on assumed sales growth and/or cost savings that are used to justify an investment initially often fail to hit the mark in the face of inevitable uncertainties of the rapid technological and competitive changes that are so pronounced in today's business environment.

As the foregoing examples suggest, we need to appreciate two fundamental aspects of ROI analysis.

The first and most important is that ROI analysis—no matter how extensive, complex, or sophisticated—is no better than the basic assumptions used in determining the amount of the investment and the anticipated earnings or savings. The second, closely related to the first, is that any accurate ROI assessment can include only those costs that are truly, objectively relevant to the investment decision being evaluated. As obvious as these simple points may seem, "relevant economics" and "realistic assumptions" are the sine qua non of any intelligent, objective analysis of a new investment.

The capital investment decision, as we have noted, usually requires an estimate of earnings in the future, and the investment to generate those benefits normally involves significant expenditure for property, plant, and/or some equipment or so-called fixed assets. These fixed assets are a monument to the future.

Should the investment prove to be unprofitable, these assets, the monument, is not easily disposed of. Furthermore, associated with the fixed assets are certain fixed costs—costs that do not vary regardless of the profitability of the investment.

Depreciation is a good example of a fixed cost. (Depreciation, as we discussed in Chapter 6, is the process of charging the estimated use, or deterioration, of an asset as an expense against the business.) Depreciation is charged over the useful life of an asset according to guidelines established by the Internal Revenue Service.

Let's assume a manufacturer has invested $1 million in a machine that has a useful life of 10 years. By using the straight-line method of depreciation (one of many methods that may be used), the manufacturer charges the business $100,000 a year over the 10-year period.

But let's suppose that after the fourth year of the machine's operation, the country's economy takes a sharp downturn and profits for all businesses sag. The manufacturer is hooked with those $100,000 yearly depreciation charges for another six years, an expense that may no longer be affordable because of the declining income. The manufacturer may decide to sell the machine, something that would be very difficult to do in a recessionary period. If he is lucky enough to find a buyer, he will undoubtedly sell the machine for a fraction of what it was worth. A bad investment is almost always a bargain for the buyer at the expense of the original investor. To grasp this point, one need only recollect that major U.S. corporations wrote off millions of dollars in prior years as they owned up to the investments that they had made during the roaring 1980s and that had gone sour in the 1990s.

The permanence of the capital investment decision distinguishes it from other types of business decisions. To make this distinction clear, let's consider another kind of investment decision—the decision to undertake a 10-year sales expansion of a product. The cost of the expansion is estimated at $1 million, and the yearly cost will be (like the depreciation charge on the machine) $100,000. But if this company were to run into bad times and its profits were to decline, all it would have to do is to reduce or eliminate the program, since the company has no money tied up in expensive machinery or buildings and is therefore free to drop the sales program and use that $100,000 for other purposes.

Another aspect of the permanence of the capital investment

decision is worth mentioning. Any capital investment decision is made within the context of a business strategy, and the impact of that decision on the total strategy should be thoroughly analyzed and evaluated before the decision is made. Once an investment decision is implemented, it binds the business to that strategy.

For example, consider the strategic implications of a decision to locate a new textile manufacturing plant in New England rather than in the South—or even in Taiwan or Mexico. In making this decision, the manufacturer must consider, not only what type of textile should be manufactured and how much of it, but these other questions:

1. Is the labor supply adequate to meet current and anticipated needs?
2. What are the current and estimated future labor costs, including benefits for employees?
3. How skilled is the labor force? How productive is it likely to be?
4. What are the current and projected tax benefits or tax costs?
5. What are the transportation costs for raw materials and finished products?
6. Are there any other advantages or disadvantages of investment in the United States as opposed to investment in foreign countries?

These are a few of the assessments that must be made concerning only a single aspect of the investment—the location of the new plant. The manufacturer must assess dozens of other factors by the time the final investment decision is made, and the company will have to live with the decision—either profitably or unprofitably—for a long, long time.

So far, we have discussed return on investment as a broad concept, stressed its importance, and touched on some of the basic steps involved in the ROI analysis process. We now begin to examine in more detail two of the three basic methods for quantifying the return on an investment—the payback method and the accounting method. (The third method, present value analysis, is the subject of Chapter 11.)

The Payback Method

As its name suggests, the **payback method** calculates the time it will take for a new investment to pay for itself. Like the method itself, the formula for calculating this time period is simple and straightforward:

$$\frac{\text{Original net investment}}{\text{Annual earnings after tax + depreciation}} = \text{Payback period}$$

To demonstrate how the formula works, let's turn to another simplified example—John Brown, who is planning to buy a new machine for his own widget manufacturing business.

> *Gross investment:* John has checked with several manufacturers and has received several bids. The machine best suited to his needs costs $17,600. The cost of delivering and installing the machine on the factory floor is $400. Thus, the total cost of the machine, including delivery and installation, is $18,000.
>
> *Salvage value of old machine:* When the new machine is installed, John will retire his old machine, which he knows he can sell for $900.
>
> *Savings relevant to new machine:* John wants to buy the new machine because it automates a step in the widget manufacturing process, thereby eliminating the services of one laborer. With the installation of the new machine, John will be able to save the wages and benefit costs for one employee, or $8,400.
>
> *Other costs associated with the new machine:* The new machine will cost about the same as the old machine to operate, so there will be no difference in operating costs. The only additional costs will be the depreciation expense (discussed in Chapter 6).

Exhibit 10-2. Return on investment: elements for payback calculation.

Gross investment	
Cost of new machine	$17,600
Delivery and installation	400
Total gross investment	$18,000
Net investment	
Gross investment	$18,000
Less salvage value for old machine	900
Total net investment	$17,100
Determination of annual depreciation costs	
Gross investment in new machines	$18,000
Less estimated salvage value at end of useful life	1,800
Net investment to be depreciated	$16,200
Estimated life of machine	9 years
Annual depreciation expense based on straight-line depreciation method $16,200 ÷ 9 years	$ 1,800
Savings as a result of new machine	
Elimination of one laborer's annual salary and benefits	$ 8,400

The first step in calculating depreciation is to estimate the useful life of the machine—let's say nine years. The second step is to estimate the machine's salvage value at the end of its useful life—let's say $1,800. The third step is to deduct the salvage value from the cost of the new machine. The remainder is the amount that must be depreciated over the life of the machine. Thus, when John deducts the estimated salvage value of $1,800 from the gross of $18,000, he is left with $16,200 to be depreciated over the nine years of the machine's life.

If he uses the straight-line method of depreciation (one of several he could choose), John will have an annual depreciation cost of $1,800. (The annual depreciation charge on the straight-line method is calculated by dividing $16,200—the value to be depreciated—by the useful life of the machine—nine years.)

All these facts, which are summarized in Exhibit 10-2, provide John with the basic information he needs to calculate the payback on his proposed investment.

In demonstrating how John calculates the payback on his investment, we will follow the steps discussed earlier in the chapter that are basic to any investment decision.

1. *Identify and Quantify Investment.* We have two choices. We can choose to use either the net investment (cost of new machine less salvage value of the old machine) or the gross investment (cost of the new machine), although the choice between these two is not nearly as important as the consistent use of that choice in subsequent investments. If John uses his net investment in calculating the payback for this investment, he must use net investment in analyzing any future investments he makes.

John does in fact decide that net investment will produce a more accurate estimate of the investment's payback period. His net investment is $17,100 ($18,000-$900 salvage value for his old machine).

2. *Determine "net" savings or earnings.* The second step in basic investment analysis is to determine the annual savings or earnings generated by the investment and to identify any new costs associated with the investment. John's new machine generates savings (rather than earnings) and incurs depreciation costs of $1,800 a year.

Salary and benefit savings from elimination of one laborer	$8,400
Less annual depreciation costs associated with new machine	1,800
Net new savings before tax	$6,600

3. *Identify tax costs and consequences.* The third step is to determine the effect of income taxes on the net savings generated by the investment. If we assume that any new income or savings generated by John's business will be taxed at 25%, we can determine the tax effect on these savings as follows:

Salary and benefit savings from elimination of one laborer	$8,400
Less annual depreciation costs associated with new machine	1,800
Net new savings before tax	$6,600
Federal income tax on new savings at 25%	1,650
Net new savings after tax	$4,950

Here it is necessary to say a few words about our tax calculations. First, we've used the 25% tax rate on the increased earnings John anticipates as a result of his savings in labor. But if Brown Widget Enterprise earns less than $50,000 a year, its earnings would be taxed at a much lower rate. John's taxable savings are reduced by the amount of his depreciation expense. Thus, his gross savings ($8,400) less the depreciation costs of the new machine ($1,800) produces taxable savings of $6,600.

The denominator in the payback equation is the net annual profits after tax plus the annual depreciation. For Brown Widget, we have the following:

New savings after tax	$4,950
Plus annual depreciation costs	1,800
Total	$6,750

Here again, some explanation is in order. As suggested by the term itself, payback refers to a time period in which an investment pays for itself, i.e., generates enough cash to recover its original costs. As we have suggested in our earlier comments, the depreciation charges do not represent a cash outlay; they are only a bookkeeping adjustment to account for the cost incurred by using an asset over its life. This is why the annual depreciation charges are added back to the annual net profit.

Thus, in our example, John expects his investment to produce gross labor savings, or cash flows, of $8,400. We have calculated that John must pay $1,650 in taxes on these savings. This leaves him with $6,750 of net cash flow. We can get the same result by adding net savings after tax to annual depreciation cost, as is shown in Exhibit 10-3.

We now have the denominator of our payback equation. Our next step is to obtain the numerator. In our example, this is simple—the numerator is simply the original net investment (the original cost of the machine, delivered and installed, less the salvage value of the old machine). Thus, the original net investment here is $17,100. The final step is simple division:

Exhibit 10-3. Determining cash flow (denominator for payback calculation).

Method I: Net after-tax savings plus depreciation	
Net savings after tax	$4,950
Plus annual depreciation costs	1,800
Total annual cash flow	$6,750
Method II: Gross cash savings less cash tax expense	
Gross cash labor savings	8,400
Less cash tax expense	1,650
Total annual cash flow	$6,750

$$\frac{\text{Original net investment}}{\text{Annual earnings after tax + annual depreciation}} = \frac{\$17,100}{\$6,750} = 2.53$$

Since our denominator is expressed as annual earnings and annual depreciation, the result of our division can be expressed in years. We can therefore say that the after-tax savings resulting from John's investment of $17,100 will pay back that investment in about two years and six months.

4. *Determine whether the investment is justified.* Without any great complexity, we have quantified the return on John's investment in terms of payback. As is true of most techniques in financial analysis, the mechanics are simple. Interpretation of the results, however, is what really counts. It's not difficult to calculate the payback period, but is two years and six months good or bad? And how does this information help John make a better investment decision?

A few thoughts come immediately to mind. First, we know that John has estimated that the machine will last nine years. If we calculate that the investment will be paid back in 2.53 years, the machine will therefore contribute the savings it generates to John's cash flow for six years and six months, more than two thirds the useful life of the machine (9 years − 2.53 years = 6.47 years). On this basis, John can conclude that the machine is a sound investment.

But what if the increased cash flow generated by the investment is not so stable? What if, for example, John plans to invest in a new product line rather than a new machine, and his estimated increased cash flows will result from the sale of the new product rather than from savings in human resources? Earnings from new product sales are obviously much less certain than are the savings generated by a new machine. Savings usually are readily identified and controlled, but sales must be increased in the face of the uncertainties of the general economy and the actions of competitors. Thus, if John were considering investing in a new product, he probably would not be so confident about the payback period. He might desire a shorter payback, or he might simply be more cautious about making the investment.

In determining the adequacy of a payback period, we also need to take into account the nature of the industry in which the investment is being made. An electric public utility, for example, can predict with relative certainty what the future demand for electrical energy will be in the area it serves. The basic demand for electrical energy is well established and stable, since electricity is a necessity. Let us assume that the widget manufacturing industry has similar characteristics. Under this set of circumstances, two years and six months does not seem to be an unduly lengthy payback period. But what if John Brown were buying a machine to make a very special, high-fashion item of women's clothing? The fashion industry is "faddy" and volatile, so John might reasonably conclude that a two-year, six-month payback is unacceptable.

How else might John use the payback method? If he were unhappy with his 2.53-year payback, he could look for other machines that might realize greater savings, perform payback calculations for each of these alternatives, and rank the machines according to their payback periods. This could help him decide which of the alternatives would produce the best return on his investment.

Finally, John might use the payback calculation to guide him in financing the investment. Let's suppose that he obtained a five-year loan for the purchase of the machine. In that case, the investment—with its two-year, six-month payback—would have already been repaid by the savings it had generated at the time the loan was due, and it would have contributed to business profits for almost two and one-half years. If the loan had been due in

Exhibit 10-4. Return on investment: elements for accounting method calculation.

Investment	
Gross investment	
Cost of new machine	$17,600
Delivery and installation	400
Total gross investment	$18,000
Net investment	
Gross investment	$18,000
Less salvage value for old machine	900
Total net investment	$17,100

two years, however, then the investment would not have generated any savings to contribute to John's cash flow. Under those circumstances, to pay back the loan when it was due John would have had to divert cash from other areas of his operations, thereby possibly straining his business's financial resources.

Thus, the payback method. As an analytical technique, it is simple, direct, and practical. (Its advantages and limitations are evaluated in Chapter 12.)

The Accounting Method

The second basic method of calculating ROI is the **accounting method**. To calculate ROI by the accounting method, it is necessary to determine the net savings or earnings after depreciation and tax costs and divide that number by the total net investment, as in the following equation:

$$\frac{\text{Net savings (earnings) after depreciation and tax}}{\text{Net investment}} = \text{return on investment}$$

To demonstrate the use of the accounting method, let's turn again to John Brown's proposed purchase of a new widget machine, which we used as the basis for our discussion of the payback method. The specific elements are the same and are summarized in Exhibit 10-4.

If we apply this information to our formula for quantifying ROI by the accounting method, we have:

$$\frac{\text{Net savings after tax}}{\text{Net investment}} = \frac{\$4,950}{\$17,100} = 28.9\%$$

Note that the numerator of the equation equals net savings after depreciation and taxes, or $4,950. In determining the numerator, depreciation costs are deducted from savings (as with the payback method) because depreciation is a tax-deductible expense and reduces the amount of tax that must be paid on the savings (or earnings) that result from the investment.

The denominator is net new investment, or $17,100. When we perform the division in the formula, we determine that the new investment will yield a return of 28.9%.

Interpretation and Evaluation

Once again, the problem is how to interpret this information. Exactly what does a 28.9% return on investment mean? And how can John use this information to make a better decision?

As with the payback method, John can calculate ROI for alternative investments and then rank them in order of the return they produce. All other things being equal, he could then select the machine that would give him the highest return.

The return as determined under the accounting method can also be compared directly with the return on investment as we defined it earlier in the chapter—the interest cost on a loan or the interest yield on a savings deposit. Thus, for example, John's 28.9% return on his investment in the machine is far more attractive than the 6% or 7% he would earn if he kept this money in a time-deposit account. The difference, of course, is that the 6% or 7% return that John would earn from the savings deposit is a certainty, whereas the return on the investment in the machine depends on the continued success of John's business and the accuracy of his assumptions on the amount of labor he can save.

The rate of return as calculated under the accounting method can also be compared with the cost of the capital used to make the investment. If John must borrow money at 10% from the bank to purchase the machine, he knows that the cost of the capital used to purchase the machine will be amply covered by the anticipated ROI.

In Chapter 12, we evaluate the advantages and some of the shortcomings of the accounting method. In the meantime, we turn to the third and more complicated method of investment evaluation—present value analysis.

11

Fundamentals of Investment Analysis: Evaluating New Investments—Present Value ROI Analysis

The present value methods of ROI analysis hinge on the basic reality that money has a "time value." This idea is neither new nor complex, but we can perhaps facilitate our understanding of the concept if at the outset we indulge in a bit of fantasy.

Assume that as you read these words you are interrupted by a phone call. When you answer, you learn that you have been chosen the winner in a promotion for the state government's new lottery. You can receive $5,000 cash immediately—or, as an alternative, you can elect to be paid $7,500 five years from now. You have a day to decide how you prefer to receive your lucky winnings. Whether $5,000 today is better or worse than $7,500 five years from now can be answered objectively only if we consider the time value of money.

When we refer to the time value of money, we simply mean that it is usually better to receive a given amount of money sooner than later. Why? Because from the beginning of civilization, payment for the use of money has been in the form of interest. Thus, understanding the relationship between time and money (that is, the time value of money) begins with nothing more complicated

Exhibit 11-1. Growth of $1,000 at 10% annual compound rate of interest.

Year	Principal Plus Interest	Annual Interest at 10%	Amount at End of Year
1	$1,000.00	$100.00	$1,100.00
2	1,100.00	110.00	1,210.00
3	1,210.00	121.00	1,331.00
4	1,331.00	133.10	1,464.10
5	1,464.00	146.41	1,610.51

than understanding an ordinary savings account. From our early childhoods—whether we are now business professionals, executives, stockholders, or bankers—we have all learned to compare our investment opportunities with the fundamental of all fundamentals: the compound interest rate return of a risk-free deposit in a savings account. Compound interest means interest paid on both the principal that we have deposited and the interest that accrues on that principal, assuming that the interest income we receive is reinvested at the same rate of interest. This is something that we all know and take for granted in connection with regular savings accounts. Compound interest rates are used to determine the value of money over time. Assume, for example, that you have $1,000, and you leave it on deposit for a period of five years at an annual rate of interest of 10%, compounded annually. The money will increase in value over time, as shown in Exhibit 11-1.

The $1,000 left on deposit at a compound annual interest rate of 10% will have grown to a total value of $1,610.51 at the end of five years—the original $1,000 of principal and $610.51 of interest.

It is a relatively easy matter to apply the simple mathematics of compounding to determine what money today will be worth in the future. Obviously, all we need to know is (a) the amount of money to be deposited today, (b) the annual (or perhaps semi-annual) rate of interest that will be used to compound the principal, and (c) how many years or months the principal will be left to earn the compound interest.

At this point, the reader should recognize that quantifying the time value of money through interest compounding, as we

Exhibit 11-2. Value of $5,000 in five years at compound annual interest of 10%.

Year	Principal Plus Interest	Annual Interest at 10%	Amount at End of Year
1	$5,000.00	$500.00	$5,500.00
2	5,500.00	550.00	6,050.00
3	6,050.00	605.00	6,655.00
4	6,655.00	665.50	7,320.50
5	7,320.50	732.05	8,052.55

have just illustrated and discussed, provides us with a mechanism to determine whether we want our fantasy lottery winnings to be $5,000 today or $7,500 five years from now. The procedures that we follow will be the same; again we will make the assumption that our deposit, the principal, will earn a 10% compound annual rate of interest. The amount of principal is the $5,000 that we have if we take our prize as an immediate cash payment. The value of this $5,000 in five years at a compound annual interest rate of 10% is calculated as in Exhibit 11-2.

At 10% compound annual interest, $5,000 will grow to $8,052.55 at the end of five years. This is $552.55 more than we would have had if we had chosen the option of receiving the lottery prize of $7,500 at the end of five years. Thus, by taking into account the time value of money—in this instance, at a rate of 10% per year—we conclude that we would be better off taking our lucky winning in the form of an immediate $5,000 cash payment.

Compound interest is the conceptual cornerstone of the time value of money, and it is the essence of present value analysis. In our use of the concept thus far, we have actually calculated the compound interest values that were relevant to our illustrations. As we have seen, this is simple enough to do, but it is hardly necessary, since precalculated compound interest calculations are readily available. (Appendix A of this book contains interest factors up to 50% for time periods up to 30 years.) A sample is shown in Exhibit 11-3.

Note that the compound interest factors are expressed on the

Exhibit 11-3. Compound interest tables for 5–10% interest over 30 years.

Year	5%	6%	7%	8%	9%	10%
1	1.050	1.060	1.070	1.080	1.090	1.100
2	1.102	1.124	1.145	1.166	1.188	1.210
3	1.156	1.191	1.225	1.260	1.295	1.331
4	1.216	1.262	1.311	1.360	1.412	1.464
5	1.276	1.338	1.403	1.469	1.539	1.611
6	1.340	1.419	1.501	1.587	1.677	1.772
7	1.407	1.504	1.606	1.714	1.828	1.949
8	1.477	1.594	1.718	1.851	1.993	2.144
9	1.551	1.689	1.838	1.999	2.172	2.358
10	1.629	1.791	1.967	2.159	2.367	2.594
11	1.710	1.898	2.105	2.332	2.580	2.853
12	1.796	2.012	2.252	2.518	2.813	3.138
13	1.886	2.133	2.410	2.720	3.066	3.452
14	1.980	2.261	2.579	2.937	3.342	3.797
15	2.079	2.397	2.759	3.172	3.642	4.177
16	2.183	2.540	2.952	3.426	3.970	4.595
17	2.292	2.693	3.159	3.700	4.328	5.054
18	2.407	2.854	3.380	3.996	4.717	5.560
19	2.527	3.026	3.617	4.316	5.142	6.116
20	2.653	3.207	3.870	4.661	5.604	6.728
25	3.386	4.292	5.427	6.848	8.632	10.835
30	4.322	5.743	7.612	10.063	13.268	17.449

basis of $1 and can thus be readily multiplied by any given amount of money. For example, a shortcut to obtaining the value of $5,000 in five years at 10% is simply to refer to the table and look for the factor for 10% at the end of five years, which is 1.611. If we multiply this by $5,000.00 (1.611 × 5,000), we get a value of $8,055.

In our calculation we actually ended up with a figure of $8,052.55. The difference between this number and the $8,055 we obtained by using the compound interest factors occurs because the value of $1 at the end of five years at 10% actually compounds to $1.61051 (1.61051 × 5,000 = 8.052.55), but in the compound interest table it is rounded off to the third digit—hence, $1.611.

Future Value vs. Present Value

We have seen how compounded interest can help us determine the future value of a current dollar. Thus, if we have $1 now, we know that in five years at 10% compound interest it will become $1.611. At 8% interest it will become $1.469 at the end of five years. At 9% it will become $1.539 after five years. (See Exhibit 11-3 or, for rates above 10%, refer to compound interest tables in Appendix A.)

Now let us turn the question around and ask how we can determine what money that we will receive in the future is worth to us *now*—in other words, what is the *present value* of money. Since we use compound interest factors to determine the future value of money we receive in the *present*, it is logical that they also be used to determine the *present value* of money that we will receive in the future. Let's be more specific. If we refer again to our compound interest table, we see that at 10% interest a dollar today will have the following values in the future:

Value today	$1.000
Value in 1 year	1.100
Value in 2 years	1.210
Value in 3 years	1.331

With these figures in front of us, let us ask again: If money is worth 10% to us, or if we can get a 10% return (interest) on it, what is the *present value* of a dollar that will be received a year from now? If at an interest rate of 10%, $1 received today will be worth $1.10 a year from now, then the value of $1 received a year from now must be the reciprocal of its future value of $1.10. The derivation of its present value at 10% is therefore carried out as follows.

$$\frac{\text{Value today}}{\text{Value a year from now}} = \frac{\$1.00}{\$1.10} = .909 \text{ (present-value reciprocal)}$$

The same procedure is used to determine the present value reciprocal at the end of the second and third years:

$$\frac{\text{Value today}}{\text{Value two years from now}} = \frac{\$1.00}{\$1.210} = .826$$

$$\frac{\text{Value today}}{\text{Value three years from now}} = \frac{\$1.00}{\$1.331} = .751$$

Let us review for a moment. Money has a time value because it is better to receive money sooner than later. Thus, as our illustration indicates, if money is worth 10% a year, the dollar we receive a year from now actually has a value of only $0.909 to us right now. If we had the dollar now and could keep it for a year, we would increase its value by the interest factor (10%). Since we do not have it now—and must wait a year to receive it—we use the interest factor to decrease its value. Another way to express the idea is to say that we have **discounted** the value of the dollar that we will receive a year from now in order to reflect the fact that we do not have it now.

We can actually prove the validity of our discounting for the present value derivation in several ways.

As we have shown, the present value of $1.00 at 10% interest received three years from now is $0.751. If this is true, then conversely we should be able to invest $0.751 today at a 10% compound interest rate and have $1 three years from now.

Year	Principal Plus Interest	Annual Interest at 10%	Amount at End of Year
1	$0.751000	0.075100	0.826100
2	0.826100	0.082610	0.908710
3	0.908710	0.090871	0.999581

Our $0.751 investment at 10% has grown to $0.999 or $1 at the end of the third year.

The validity of the discounting process can be seen from another perspective—namely, the absolute reciprocal relationship between compound interest factors and present value factor, or, as we have referred to them, present value derivations. This point is illustrated using a 10% interest rate.

Exhibit 11-4. Present value table for 6–14% interest over 10 years.

Year	6%	8%	10%	12%	14%
1	0.943	0.926	0.909	0.893	0.877
2	0.890	0.857	0.826	0.797	0.769
3	0.840	0.794	0.751	0.712	0.675
4	0.792	0.735	0.683	0.636	0.592
5	0.747	0.681	0.621	0.567	0.519
6	0.705	0.630	0.564	0.507	0.456
7	0.665	0.583	0.513	0.452	0.400
8	0.627	0.540	0.467	0.404	0.351
9	0.592	0.500	0.424	0.361	0.308
10	0.558	0.463	0.386	0.322	0.270

(In general terms, "reciprocal" is defined as inversely related. The technical mathematical definition, taken from Webster's *New World Dictionary*, is "the quantity resulting from the division of 1 by the given quantity; a quantity which, when multiplied by the given quantity, equals 1. Example: the reciprocal of 7 is 1/7.")

Time Period	Compound Interest Factor		Present Value Factor		Reciprocal
0	1.00	×	1.000	=	1
1	1.10	×	.909	=	1
2	1.21	×	.826	=	1
3	1.33	×	.751	=	1

Discounting, therefore, is reverse compounding. Indeed, we can simply use a compound interest factor to calculate the reciprocal present value factor or derivation. Although these calculations may help demonstrate the relationship between these two concepts, such labor is necessary only for purposes of illustration. Precalculated present value tables are readily available and are shown in Appendix B of this book for interest rates from 1% to 30% over a period of 30 years. Exhibit 11-4 demonstrate that the factors for 10% are exactly the same as those we calculated.

Exhibit 11-5. Calculating the present value of $7,500 paid in five installments of $1,500 each.

Time Period (Year)	Money Received	Present Value Factor at 10%	Present Value of Money Received
1	$1,500	0.909	$1,363.50
2	1,500	0.826	1,239.00
3	1,500	0.751	1,126.50
4	1,500	0.683	1,024.50
5	1,500	0.621	931.50
Total	$7,500		$5,685.00

The concepts and techniques of present value analysis allow us to quantify the benefit of money we expect to receive in the future compared with the value of money today. This was our problem at the outset of the chapter, when we had to decide whether we wanted our prize to be $5,000 today or $7,500 five years from now. We were able to answer that question by taking into account the time value of money. We can get the same answer by means of a present value analysis. Thus, the question becomes: If money is worth 10%, what is the present value of $7,500 received five years from now? To determine this, we look at our present value table and find that the present value of $1 received at the end of five years at 10% interest is $0.621. If $1 has a present value of $0.621, then the $7,500 we would expect to receive is worth $4,657.50 (0.621 × $7,500 = $4,657.50) today. This $4,657.50 is less than the $5,000 we can receive as an immediate (*present*) cash prize. We should obviously opt for the $5,000 now.

Through the use of present value analysis, we are able to look at different amounts of money received at different times and compare them. By way of further illustration, let us assume we are being given the option to receive the $7,500 prize in five annual installments of $1,500 each. How would we feel about this alternative to a $5,000 immediate cash payment? Once again, we need to take into account the value of money, as shown in Exhibit 11-5.

Under this alternative, our prize would have a present value of $5,685 and would thus be more valuable than $5,000, the present value of an immediate cash payment.

Understanding the time value of money and the techniques of quantity is important. They are always present in the various methods of determining the return on an investment taking into account the present value of the money generated as savings or earnings by an investment.

The principal difference between present value methods of ROI analysis and the accounting and payback methods discussed in Chapter 10 is that the present value methods take into account the time value of money. (Please note that when we speak of the "time value of money," we refer literally to cold, hard cash.) Thus, all methods of present value ROI analysis deal only with cash inflows or outflows associated with an investment. In addition, because present value methods take into account the value of money in relation to time, the cash inflows or outflows must be identified by a time period—that is, do they take place in the first, second, fifth, or eighth year of the investment project?

The first step in any ROI analysis is to identify the investment. With the present value methods, the investment must be identified in reference to cash and to when the investment takes place (one year, two years, and so on). The same is true in analyzing "savings" under present value methods. Savings, including tax effects, are only cash savings and must be identified by time period. Thus, if the cash savings are $3,000 for the first year and $2,000 for the second year, they should be recorded as such.

To illustrate these points more specifically, let us return to the investment/savings profile of Brown Widget Enterprise, used in Chapter 10.

The Cash Investment

Because we will use present value methods of ROI analysis, all these elements must be evaluated exclusively in terms of their cash impact. First let's look at our investment. The cost of the new machine is $17,600, and this will be paid in cash. It is therefore a cash outflow. The delivery and installation cost must also be paid for in cash. Thus, we can identify a total of $18,000 of cash outflow associated with the gross investment. We also noted, however, that John Brown expects to receive another cash payment of $900 for the salvage value of the old machine that is being replaced. This $900 reduces the total net investment to $17,100—the true cash outflow associated with the investment. Furthermore, all these cash outflows will take place within essentially the same period of time and will be treated accordingly in our calculations. If in fact the investment were to be made over a period of two years, this would also have to be taken into account.

The Cash Savings

As a result of the investment in the new machine, we calculated that the net savings or net improvement after taxes to the profitability of John Brown's business would be as follows:

Salary and benefit savings from elimination of one laborer	$8,400
Less annual depreciation costs associated with new machine	1,800
Net new savings before tax	$6,600
Less federal income tax on new savings at 25%	$1,650
Net new savings after tax	$4,950

The net new savings after tax have taken into account the effect of the annual depreciation costs that will result from the new machine. These depreciation expenses need to be considered in order to determine the effect of the investment on net income, or profit. As we noted in Chapter 6, however, depreciation is a cost that arises only from an accounting adjustment and not from a cash payment. Thus, the $4,950 of net new savings does not represent the cash savings that we must identify for our analysis with a present value method. This cash savings can be pinpointed—just as in the case of the payback method—by adding the $1,800 of "noncash" depreciation charges to the $4,950 of net new savings. The result is as follows:

Net new savings after tax	$4,950
Plus annual depreciation costs	1,800
Total annual cash flows or earnings	$6,750

The annual cash flow or cash earnings of $6,750 represents the same number that we used in the denominator for our payback calculation in Chapter 10. You will recall that the payback method also seeks to isolate the "cash effect," since it attempts to determine how much cash will be generated in order to pay back the investment. Finally, we might also note that, as is almost always the case, federal income taxes on the new savings are assumed to be a cash expense associated with the investment. Here again, however, if this were not the case—that is, if for some reason these taxes could be deferred for payment in later years—this would also need to be taken into account in our present value analysis.

Earlier we pointed out that in attempting to identify the cash elements in a present value ROI analysis, it is often useful to think in terms of "flows." Cash almost always flows out to make the investment and subsequently flows in as a result of the net new savings or earnings. But there is one particular element of cash flow that merits special attention in present value analysis: residual income cash flows.

Residual Income Cash Flows

The total gross investment in the new widget-forming machine, including installation, is $18,000. Because we received $900 as scrap value for the old machine, however, our net investment was reduced to $17,100. Almost without exception, used equipment or machinery can be disposed of for some value. For this same reason, when we calculated the total cost of the new machine that we have to depreciate over its expected useful life of nine years, it, too, had a salvage value. We assumed that this salvage value would be $1,800 and accordingly reduced our original $18,000 cost to $16,200.

The economic fact of life that almost all assets have some

terminal or residual value at the end of their useful lives is recognized in computing depreciation costs and also in all present value methods of ROI analysis. This is called the **residual value assumption,** which is nothing more than an assumption about what cash payment can be expected for an asset at the end of that asset's useful life. As a general approach, the residual value of an asset is generally assumed to be the same as its expected final salvage value (although we should note that in today's economy, the tendency for tangible property to appreciate or hold its value has perhaps made this rather simplistic and conventional approach somewhat anachronistic). Under this method, the residual value assumption for the widget-forming machine is the $1,800 that we have estimated as its salvage value. As we will see in subsequent illustrations, this residual value is assumed to be a cash inflow at the end of the investment's or project's economic life.

With these general points in mind, we can now examine the first of three basic methods of present value ROI analysis—the present value method.

The Present Value Method

Under the **present value** method, an investment proposal is acceptable if, apart from nonmonetary considerations, the present value of cash earnings at the desired rate of return is greater than or equal to the investment that is being made to generate the savings or earnings. The procedures for developing the computation to determine whether an investment is acceptable under the present value method can be summarized as follows:

1. Estimate the future cash outflows and inflows associated with the capital investment proposal for each specific year of the project's or investment's expected life.

2. Determine the rate of return desired for the project. (In Chapter 13, we explore the various approaches to selecting such a rate; for illustrative purposes, we will choose arbitrary rates in the following examples.)

3. Refer to the present value tables (Appendix B) to choose the correct present value factors under the rate of return that has

been selected. Note that different present value factors will be required for each year.

4. Calculate the present value of the cash inflows (savings) for each year by multiplying them by the present value factors for that year.

5. Add the total amount of the present value of each year's inflow for the life of the project. If the amount equals or exceeds the amount of the investment, that investment will be acceptable. If the sum of the net present value of the cash flows for each year is less than the amount of the investment, the investment will be unacceptable.

6. Bear in mind that nonmonetary considerations have been ignored. Make certain it is safe to do this. Also recognize that the validity of all these sophisticated calculations is no more accurate than the assumptions that underlie the estimates of investment or savings.

Now let us turn to an actual application of these procedures, again using our illustration of the investment in the widget-forming machine. The elements of our ROI analysis for this project under the present value method are set forth in Exhibit 11-6.

According to the procedures that we outlined above, the investment analysis under the present value method at our arbitrarily designated 20% rate of return appears in Exhibit 11-7.

The total present value of all the cash savings (inflows) that are assumed for nine years, including the assumed cash residual value, amounts to $27,560, which is $10,460 greater than the amount of our cash investment of $17,100. Therefore, under our present value decision rule, we can conclude that the investment is justified, since the present value of the savings (the cash inflows) exceeds the cash outflows associated with the investment at the desired rate of return of 20%.

For contrast, we will now follow exactly the same procedures, but in this instance we will set our desired rate of return at 30%. At this earnings rate, our present value analysis results in the figures shown in Exhibit 11-8.

As the calculations indicate, the expected cash savings or cash inflows, discounted at a present value factor of 30%, give a total present value of $20,541, which is $3,441 more than the $17,100

Exhibit 11-6. Elements of ROI calculation—present value method.

Investment (outflows)	
Cost of new machine—cash outflow	$17,600
Delivery and installation—cash outflow	400
Total gross investment—cash outflow	$18,000
Less salvage value of old machine—cash inflow	900
Total net investment—net cash outflow	$17,100
Cash savings (inflows)	
Net new savings after tax	$ 4,950
Plus annual noncash depreciation costs	1,800
Total annual cash savings (inflows)	$ 6,750
Estimated project life (same as estimated life of machine)	9 years
Residual value	
Assumed to be estimate salvage value at end of machine's useful life (same as for depreciation calculation)—cash inflow in ninth year	$ 1,800
Desired earnings rate (arbitrary figure)	20%

investment. Therefore, under our present value decision rule, the project is still acceptable.

These two examples provide a useful illustration of (1) the application of the decision rule for the present value method in a positive situation at different rates of return; and (2) the mechanical procedures that are followed to arrive at the ROI calculation under the present value method. These two examples also highlight the critical importance of the choice of the desired rate of return.

Now we will look at the second basic method of present value ROI analysis—the discounted cash flow or the internal rate of return method.

Discounted Cash Flow— Internal Rate of Return

Discounted cash flow and **internal rate of return** are two different names for exactly the same method of ROI analysis. Discounted

Exhibit 11-7. Calculation by present value method of ROI in widget-forming machine (desired rate of return, 20%).

Year	Item	Cash-flow Effect Outflows/ Inflows (dollars)	Present Value Factor at 20%		Present Value of Investments Outflows (dollars)	Present Value of Cash Flows Savings, Inflows (dollars)
	Investment	(17,100)	× 1.000	=	(17,100)	
1	Cash savings	6,750	× 0.833	=		5,623
2	Cash savings	6,750	× 0.694	=		4,685
3	Cash savings	6,750	× 0.579	=		3,908
4	Cash savings	6,750	× 0.482	=		3,254
5	Cash savings	6,750	× 0.402	=		2,714
6	Cash savings	6,750	× 0.335	=		2,261
7	Cash savings	6,750	× 0.279	=		1,883
8	Cash savings	6,750	× 0.233	=		1,573
9	Cash savings	6,750	× 0.194	=		1,310
	Assumed cash residual value	1,800	× 0.194	=		349
Totals:	Investment				(17,100)	
	Savings					27,560

cash flow is also often expressed by the acronym DCF. (A waggish student of ROI once suggested that the term more appropriately stood for "Don't Comprehend Fully," although it is hoped that the following discussion will refute this allegation.)

The basic difference between the present value method that we looked at earlier and the DCF-internal rate of return method is that under the DCF/IRR approach, the analyst has to find a present value factor that will discount the expected future outflows so that they will equal the investment, given the present value of money. The decision rule, therefore, for the DCF/IRR method can be stated as follows:

An investment proposal is acceptable if, apart from nonmonetary considerations, the present value of the

Exhibit 11-8. Calculation by present value method of ROI in widget-forming machine (desired rate of return, 30%).

Year	Item	Cash-flow Effect Outflows/ Inflows (dollars)		Present Value Factor at 30%		Present Value of Investments Outflows (dollars)	Present Value of Cash Flows Savings, Inflows (dollars)
	Investment	(17,100)	×	1.000	=	(17,100)	
1	Cash savings	6,750	×	0.769	=		5,191
2	Cash savings	6,750	×	0.592	=		3,996
3	Cash savings	6,750	×	0.455	=		3,071
4	Cash savings	6,750	×	0.350	=		2,363
5	Cash savings	6,750	×	0.269	=		1,816
6	Cash savings	6,750	×	0.207	=		1,397
7	Cash savings	6,750	×	0.159	=		1,073
8	Cash savings	6,750	×	0.123	=		830
9	Cash savings	6,750	×	0.094	=		635
	Assumed cash residual value	1,800	×	0.094	=		169
Totals:	Investment					(17,100)	
	Savings						20,541

cash earnings or inflow equals the investment at a present value factor—or a rate of return—that is considered acceptable.

Because under the DCF/IRR method a rate of return must be found and then a determination made as to whether it is acceptable, the procedures used in the computation vary greatly from those used in the present value method. They are as follows:

1. The estimated future net cash outflows and inflows to be derived from the capital investment proposal are identified year by year (just as in the present value method).

2. A present value factor, which it is believed will discount

the future cash savings (inflows) so that they will equal the investment, is estimated. (Note that there is no other way to approach this than to use a simple trial-and-error method.)

3. Once an approximate present value factor has been identified, the next higher or lower present value factor is used to discount the cash savings, following the same method. From these two "bridging" calculations, the exact rate that would make the cash savings equal the investment should be interpolated. (An explanation and illustration of this interpolation procedure follows this exposition.)

To illustrate these procedures, we will again use our widget-forming example. All the elements for our ROI analysis are the same, and the return on investment calculation under the DCF/IRR method is illustrated in Exhibit 11-9.

Interpolating an Exact Return Rate With the DCF/IRR Method

We want the exact rate (present value factor) that discounts cash savings to exactly $17,100 of investment. At a rate of 35%, cash savings are discounted to a total present value of $18,111. At 40%, cash savings are discounted to a total present value of $16,139. Therefore, the exact rate must be somewhere between 35% and 40%, and the 5% difference between those two rates results in a $1,972 difference in the present value of the cash savings.

Present value cash savings at 35%	$18,111
Present value cash savings at 40%	16,139
Difference	$ 1,972

The difference between the amount of $17,100 to which we want to discount *exactly* and the total amount of the present value of the cash earnings at 35% is $1,011.

Exhibit 11-9. Calculation of ROI in widget-forming machine (DCF/IRR method).

Year	Item	Cash Flow Effect (Outflow)/ Inflow (in dollars)	Present Value Factor at 35%		Present Value of Cash Flows Investment Savings (in dollars) (Outflows)	Inflows	Cash Flow Effect (Outflow)/ Inflow (in dollars)	Present Value Factor at 40%		Present Value of Cash Flows Investment Savings (in dollars) (Outflows)	Inflows
	Investment	(17,100)	1.000	×	(17,100)		(17,100)	1.000	×	(17,100)	
1	Cash savings	6,750	0.741	×		5,002	6,750	0.714	×		4,820
2	Cash savings	6,750	0.549	×		3,706	6,750	0.510	×		3,443
3	Cash savings	6,750	0.406	×		2,741	6,750	0.364	×		2,457
4	Cash savings	6,750	0.301	×		2,032	6,750	0.260	×		1,755
5	Cash savings	6,750	0.223	×		1,505	6,750	0.186	×		1,256
6	Cash savings	6,750	0.165	×		1,114	6,750	0.133	×		898
7	Cash savings	6,750	0.122	×		824	6,750	0.095	×		641
8	Cash savings	6,750	0.091	×		614	6,750	0.068	×		459
9	Cash savings	6,750	0.067	×		452	6,750	0.048	×		324
	Assumed cash residual value	1,800	0.067	×		121	1,800	0.048	×		86
Totals:	Investment				(17,100)					(17,100)	
	Savings					18,111					16,139

Present value cash savings at 35%	$18,111
Amount to which we want to exactly discount	17,100
Difference	$ 1,011

The ratio between these two is .513—1,011 divided by 1,972 equals 51.3%. Thus, 51.3% of the 5% rate difference will give us the exact rate (present value factor) that will discount the cash savings to $17,100. This rate is 35% plus 2.57%, or 37.57%.

Thus, the widget-forming machine has an estimated rate of return of 37.52%. This is the rate on the present value factor that discounted the future cash savings so that it equaled the investment. Since we have already said that a return of 20% is acceptable, the widget-forming machine with its 37.57% return meets this requirement and can be approved. Assume that we now insist upon a 40% return. Using this criterion, the project's expected 37.57% percentage return is *not* acceptable, and the project will be rejected. Note again the importance of the desired rate of return for the decision process—although in this case it occurred a step later than it did under the simple present value method.

Excess Present Value Index

Let us conclude by taking a brief look at a third and final variation on the use of present value ROI techniques—the excess present value (EPV) index. As we have discussed, the DCF/IRR method expresses ROI as a single percentage; if that rate of return is found to be acceptable, the entire project will then be judged acceptable. In certain instances, the exclusive use of the DCF/IRR approach can lead to erroneous conclusions. When this is the case, the EPV indexing method is a useful supplementary tool.

Assume, for example, that we have an opportunity to invest in one, but only one, of two projects. Project A calls for an investment of $1,000 and has estimated cash earnings (including residual cash values) of $1,200 for one year. The present value factor that discounts this $1,200 back to the $1,000 of investment is $0.833

Exhibit 11-10. Project B: ROI calculation (DCF/IRR method).

Year	Item	Cash Flow Effect (Outflows) Inflows (in dollars)	Present Value Factor at 15%	Present Value of Cash Flows Investment/Savings (in dollars)
	Investment	(1,000)		(1,000)
1	Cash savings	300	0.870	261.00
2	Cash savings	300	0.756	227.00
3	Cash savings	300	0.658	197.40
4	Cash savings	300	0.572	171.60
5	Cash savings	300	0.497	149.10
Totals			(1,000)	1,006.10

($1,200 × 0.833 = $999.60 or $1,000), which indicates a return of 20%.

Project B also calls for an investment of $1,000 and has estimated cash earnings (including residual cash values) of $300 per year for five years. As the calculations in Exhibit 11-10 show, a present value factor of 15% is found to discount these cash earnings back to the investment of $1,000.

On the basis of the DCF/IRR method, Project A appears preferable, since it supposedly has a return of 20% versus one of 15% for Project B. However, let us suppose that upon further consideration we conclude that a 10% rate of return is acceptable. The cash earnings for both projects are now discounted at this rate and are as they are shown in Exhibit 11-11.

The next step, then, is to employ the EPV Index, which involves nothing more than indexing the two investments in terms of the relationship of the present value of the expected earnings to the investment at this 10% rate. As shown in Exhibit 11-12, Project A has an EPV index of 1.09, whereas Project B has an index of 1.14. Under such an index comparison, Project B appears to be more attractive than Project A.

We can appreciate exactly the same point by recognizing that

Exhibit 11-11. Comparison of cash earnings of Project A vs. Project B at 10% present value factor.

Year	Cash Savings (in dollars)	Present Value Factor at 10%	Present Value of Cash Earnings*
		Project A	
1	1,200.00	0.909	1,091
Total			1,091
		Project B	
1	300.00	0.909	273
2	300.00	0.826	248
3	300.00	0.751	225
4	300.00	0.683	205
5	300.00	0.621	186
Total			1,137

* Rounded to the nearest dollar.

Exhibit 11-12. Excess present value index, Project A vs. Project B.

EPV Index (excess present value of earnings/investment)

Project A

$$\frac{\text{Present value of cash earnings at 10\%}}{\text{Investment}} = \frac{\$1,091}{\$1,000} \qquad 1.09$$

Project B

$$\frac{\text{Present value of cash earnings at 10\%}}{\text{Investment}} = \frac{\$1,137}{\$1,000} \qquad 1.137$$

at the 10% discount factor, Project B will yield $1,137 of present value earnings, whereas Project A will yield only $1,091.

As the foregoing examples suggest, the excess present value index method is a useful supplementary analytical tool when alternative investments need to be compared in the face of limited funds available for investment.

12

Fundamentals of Investment Analysis: Evaluating New Investments

In this chapter we review some of the advantages and limitations of the three basic methods for estimating ROI that we discussed in Chapters 10 and 11.

The Payback Method

Undoubtedly, the strongest advantage of the payback method is its simplicity. It is quick and easy to calculate and not difficult to understand. For these reasons, it is an excellent but rough device for a preliminary screening of many capital investment proposals.

The payback method evaluates investments in terms of time, estimating how long it will take to recoup the initial investment. This technique can be very useful where high technology, style, or economic risks are involved. Different industries require different payback periods; although a 10-year payback may be quite satisfactory to a public utility, it would probably be totally unacceptable to a computer manufacturer.

The payback method emphasizes cash recoverability of an investment, an emphasis that becomes more and more important as the cost of borrowing money constantly increases. Also, simply as a result of the methodology, the payback method gives weight only to those cash flows that occur at the beginning of the project. As we shall see later, this is also a limitation, but it is certainly in line with the general concept of the time value of money.

In the same way, of course, present value methods show much more precisely the greater value of cash earnings received in the early years of a project. In a sense, the payback method takes into account the time value of money very crudely; however, it does not fully measure the time-money rate of return as present value methods do. Furthermore, it totally ignores the profits and cash inflows that occur after the investment has been repaid. The residual values or cash flows are also overlooked. This particular shortcoming can be critical in a long-term investment. Thus, the payback method is an inadequate tool for evaluating the many investments that are long term and that are important to a company's future growth.

As a final point, we should note that, however useful it is to evaluate an investment in terms of the time period in which it will be paid back, this measurement ignores any expression of projectability or of absolute dollars. It is difficult, therefore, to compare or rank meaningfully alternative capital investments with the payback method.

In summary, the advantages and limitations of the payback methods are these:

Advantages

1. It is easy to calculate and understand
2. It provides good rough indicator for preliminary investment screening
3. It measures cash recoverability
4. It helps evaluate the risk associated with investments in terms of time until payback. Time expression can help evaluate investment in terms of risk
5. It appropriately emphasizes earlier cash flows

Limitations

1. It does not truly take into account the time value of money

2. It does not consider benefit of earnings after investment has been repaid
3. It has limited use as a tool to compare and rank alternative investments

The Accounting Method

The accounting method of ROI analysis is also sometimes referred to as the **book rate of return method.** Either designation suggests the key feature of the method—that it measures ROI in terms of standard accounting procedure and technique. This particular feature is not without benefit, since the ultimate *raison d'être* for any investment, even for an employee washroom, is increased profitability. The accounting method of investment analysis helps keep this point in focus. It also facilitates capital investments postmortems in order to determine whether the actual profitability of new investments is in line with the original estimates.

Although the accounting method makes use of standard accounting methods that might be somewhat confusing to a neophyte, it is also easy to calculate and understand. The method, however, suffers from the same limitation as the payback method in that it does not in any way recognize the time value of money; indeed, it gives no weight to either the amounts or the timing of cash flows. Finally, the methodology implicitly assumes that the investment and the associated savings or earnings will last for the depreciable life of the investment involved. In today's dynamic and volatile business environment, this can be a highly tenuous assumption. A machine that molds plastic *Star Wars* toys may last for 15 years; whether the faddish demand for such products will last that long is another question. The advantages and limitations of the accounting method are these:

Advantages

1. It emphasizes accounting profit and loss effect of investment.
2. It is consistent with, and relates to, accounting data.
3. It is easy to calculate.

Limitations

1. It does not recognize the time value of money.
2. It assumes that investment and benefits will last for the depreciable life of the assets involved.
3. It does not give any weight to amounts or timing of cash flows.

Present Value Methods

The key feature, and the advantage, of the present value methods of ROI analysis is that, unlike the other methods, present value methods take into account the time value of money. But there are other advantages to present value analysis, as is shown in the following excerpts from Robert Heller's wry, witty book *The Great Executive Dream* (New York: Delacorte Press, 1972):

> Businesses and heads of corporations don't earn profits: they earn money. Profit is an abstraction from the true, underlying movement of cash in and cash out. Any small businessman who has had trouble meeting the payroll knows the painful principle: without enough cash, you drown. Larger businessmen have learned the same lesson in the same brutal way: the mighty Penn Central in the U.S. ran out of hard currency; so did Rolls-Royce; so did a one-time British textile star, Klinger. . . . A big company's check's can rebound just as high as those of a little shopkeeper. But many top executives, even in suave and sophisticated organizations, have never mastered the truth that what counts at the end of the day is the cash in the kitty—not the abstractions in the books.

Heller's points seem well taken. They have led to a general preference for the use of present value methods as a tool for investment analysis. Present value methods not only concentrate exclusively on cash; they also give weight to the amounts and timing of all cash flows, including residual values, for the entire life of the project. This aspect gives present value methods an advantage in evaluating long-term capital investment projects. These methods also allow projects to be compared or ranked more easily by means of the excess present value index. Finally, the methodology makes it easier to account for the real versus the depreciable life of an investment project. As we pointed out earlier, the depreciable life of a machine that makes plastic *Star Wars* toys may be 15 years; the true economic life, the period over which these toys can be sold, may be only three years.

Ironically, the very real strengths of the present value methods give rise to some of their limitations. The methods are extremely sophisticated, but they are much more difficult to understand than the other two methods. Indeed, the sophistication of the present value methods can give an aura of precision and validity to investment analysis that is unwarranted, given the risk and uncertainty of basic underlying assumptions. Furthermore, if done manually, calculation of the present value methods is much more difficult and time-consuming than are the calculations for the payback and the accounting methods (particularly for the DCF/IRR methods, which require "finding" the rate of return).

Present value methods center attention on the rate of interest which equals the value of all future cash inflows and outflows. The theory is, "a dollar today is worth more than a dollar in the future." The resulting computations of discounted cash flows in the future do not directly relate to actual accounting profit and loss results, since these accounting results are presented on a non-discounting basis and are therefore not comparable.

A final limitation of all present value methods is that the methodology implicitly assumes that all cash flows from an investment can be reinvested at the rates of return that were used either to determine the desired rate of return, as in the present value method, or—as in the case of the DCF/IRR—to discount the cash flows. Let us make the point another way. The investor faces a future that begins with an outlay of funds. At the moment of decision, his or her concern is with return on that particular investment. We can assume that the return on that particular investment is equal to the rate of return indicated, but only if the investor is able to put the cash inflows from the investment back to work at the same rate of return.

It is important to understand the implicit reinvestment assumption in all the present value methods; in the same way, the accounting method implicitly assumes that the benefits of an investment will last for the entire depreciable life of the assets involved. The present value methods' implicit reinvestment assumption should be borne in mind when you are evaluating investment projects that show extraordinarily high rates of return.

The advantages and limitations of the present value methods are as follows:

Advantages

1. They measure time value of money.
2. They concentrate on cash and gives weight to both timing and amount of cash flows.
3. They facilitate ranking and comparison of investment projects.

Limitations

1. They are difficult to calculate and understand.
2. They do not readily relate to accounting—procedures, especially profit and loss effects.
3. They assume that cash flows can be reinvested at the same rate of return to discount the project.

Choosing the Best Method

Which is the best method? As we suggested earlier, most professionals would probably prefer, or in some cases even insist on, the present value methods. Yet all the methods have some advantages as well as limitations; as always, the most important element in any method of analysis is just plain common business sense. Since the capital investment decision is such an important one, it is probably well worth the effort to use all three methods.

13

Setting the Rate of Return

We have reviewed the importance of ROI and have evaluated the three basic methods of calculating it. In this chapter, we discuss how to set the rate of return and how to determine what is a good or acceptable rate of return on a new capital investment. The question is hardly academic. You may recall that the decision rule for the present value method states that a project is acceptable if, apart from nonmonetary considerations, the present value of the cash savings at the desired rate of return equals or exceeds the investment. But how do we determine a desirable rate of return? What factors should we consider? If an investment shows an expected rate of return of 8%, is this acceptable? If so, why?

Setting the rate of return is sometimes called setting the "hurdle rate," since it becomes the rate of return that all investments must "hurdle" or clear if they are to be found acceptable. There are a variety of ways to set a hurdle rate, but the first is probably the most obvious. We have referred to it often; in Chapter 11 we called it the fundamental of all fundamentals—the compound interest rate of return on a risk-free deposit in an ordinary savings account. We also observed that from our earliest childhoods—whether we are now business professionals, executives, stockholders, or bankers—we have always ultimately compared our investment opportunities with the rate of interest that we can get from an ordinary savings account.

Interest rates and yields vary over time, but at any given time the cost of borrowing money and the rate paid for money in essentially risk-free investments suggest the hurdle rate that should be set for an investment. The reasons for this are almost self-evident. If the effortless risk-free deposit of money in a savings account will yield a return of 5.47%, why pursue a business or capital investment that returns less? Also, if funds for an investment must be borrowed at 11.5%, it hardly makes sense to use them for an investment that has a return of only 6%. In this case, the cost of financing the investment would exceed the income that could be expected from it—hardly sound business practice.

Inflation, of course, has a significant influence on interest rates and yields and in and of itself is an appropriate factor to consider when you are setting a hurdle rate. If a proposed investment has a return of 10% but the value of money is declining through inflation at approximately this same rate, then any real return is illusory.

There are several other relatively simple ways to set a hurdle rate. An established company or a division can use its historical ROI performance as a hurdle rate. If the historical relationship of a company's net profits to its assets has yielded a 14% return on investment, then new investments that show a projected return of 10% will decrease rather than improve the company's overall return on investment.

A company can also set a hurdle rate in relation to competitors' or industry rates of return. Since ROI is such a basic and common measure of business performance, current and historical ROI data for all publicly traded corporations are readily available.

Although there is a variety of ready reference points that companies or investors can use to establish their hurdle rates, they can, of course, simply resort to an arbitrary or intuitive standard. In this case, they simply say that they won't make a capital investment unless it has a 25% return. If successful, this approach can bring about an improvement in the productivity (the return) on capital. There is always the risk, however, that the intuitive or arbitrary rate may be unrealistically high, with the result that no new capital investments are undertaken. The long-term business consequences of failing to make any capital investment can be disastrous.

A somewhat more complex way of establishing a hurdle rate is by using the cost of capital method. We alluded to this technique earlier in our discussion when we pointed out that it obviously makes no sense for a business to borrow money at an annual cost of 10% and then use it to make an investment whose return is 6%. As this example suggests, the basic notion of the cost of capital method is that a company's minimum hurdle rate should equal the cost of its capital. At first blush this might suggest nothing more than identifying current interest costs as the appropriate investment hurdle rate. The British economist Lord Keynes expressed much the same thought when he said, "Businessmen would continue to invest as long as the return on one more dollar of investment (marginal efficiency of capital) exceeded the interest rate (marginal cost of capital)." It seems obvious that an investment yielding 25% on funds at an interest cost of 12% is a highly attractive proposition.

If, however, we define the cost of capital only as current interest costs, we have implicitly assumed that borrowed funds are the only source of capital for a business. Such an assumption is unrealistic, since every business needs some permanent capital in the form of equity. As a matter of fact, the solvency of a publicly held corporation is constantly evaluated in terms of the relationship of debt (usually long-term debt, or obligations in excess of one year) to equity. A previously accepted rule of thumb in U.S. business is that the owners or shareholders should have $2 invested for every $1 of debt. This changes as liquidity changes both within a company and/or according to general economic conditions. The credit of companies that do not meet such standards is considered to be weaker than the credit of those that do; this weakness in turn increases the interest rates at which the companies can borrow money. These few brief comments ignore the often extensive and complex financial analyses that are used to establish and monitor a company's credit worthiness; they do, however, serve to make the point that is basic to our discussion—namely, that the cost of capital must also take into consideration the cost of equity capital. The calculation of a company's overall cost of capital, therefore, begins with an assessment of its long-term planned capital structure, including both debt and equity.

The next step involves calculating the after-tax cost of both kinds of capital. In the case of borrowed or debt capital, the calculation is relatively straightforward. If the interest cost on long-term debt is 10%, then the after-tax cost is 5.2%. (Interest expense on long-term debt at 10% is taxed at the current tax rate, 48%, leaving an after-tax cost of 5.2%.)

The calculation of the **cost of equity capital** is both more controversial and more complex. Still, most theoreticians and practitioners agree that the basic cost is derived from the relationship between a company's **earnings per share** and the **market price** at which a share of the company's stock is publicly traded. Thus, if a company's stock has an earnings per share of $1 and it sells at a prices of $10, then its cost of equity capital is 10%. The mathematical derivation of these relationships is as follows:

$$\frac{\text{Earnings per share}}{\text{Market value per share}} = \frac{\$ 1.00}{\$10.00} = 10\% \text{ (cost of equity capital)}$$

The reader may readily recognize that the cost of capital is simply the conventional earnings per share multiple shown for every publicly traded common stock, expressed as a percentage. The essence of the relationship, however, is that for a given company in a particular industry, a certain amount of earnings will attract a certain amount of capital. In our illustration, $1 of earnings attracted $10 of capital. We will discuss some of the nuances and anomalies of price/earnings relationships later, but for now let us examine how we use that relationship along with conventional interest costs to calculate the overall total cost of capital to a company.

As we have said, the first step is to define the expected long-term capital structure of the company, which for the purpose of illustration we shall assume conforms to the conventional ratio of $2 of equity for every $1 of debt. Thus, we have:

Long-term debt	$1,000,000
Shareholders' equity	2,000,000
Total	$3,000,000

If we assume that the before-tax interest cost on the debt is 10% and that the company's stock sells at the same price/earnings ratio of 10:1 that we used in our earlier illustration, then the company's overall cost of capital would be calculated as shown below:

Type of Capital	Amount	Weighted % by Total
Debt	$1,000,000	33%
Equity	2,000,000	67%
Total	$3,000,000	100%

Step 1: Calculate the weight of debt to equity in the total long-term capital structure.

Step 2: Calculate the after-tax cost of each form of capital.

1. Interest on long-term debt is a tax-deductible expense. Thus, 10% interest cost is reduced by taxes of 48% (or 4.8%), giving an after-tax cost of debt of 5.2%.

2. If the company has earnings per share of common stock at $1 and is publicly traded at $10 per share, then the cost of equity capital is 10%. The cost of this equity capital, however, is 10% on an *after-tax* basis, since the earnings per share are expressed in the form of net earnings *after tax*.

Step 3: Calculate the weighted after-tax cost of total capital for the company.

Type of Capital	Amount	Weighted % of Total	After-Tax Cost	Weighted Cost %
Debt	$1,000,000	33%	5.2%	1.7%
Equity	2,000,000	67%	10.0%	6.7%
Total	$3,000,000	100%		8.4%

The overall cost of capital after taxes, as we have calculated it, can serve as a hurdle rate below which a company should not accept an investment proposal. If it were to do so, the cost of financing the investment would be greater than the return.

We should note that the 8.4% rate may seem low; however,

this is an after-tax rate. Expressed on a before-tax basis, with tax rates of 48%, for example, it would nearly double to 16.2% (8.4% ÷ 52% = 16.15%). As we noted earlier, we also need to consider the price/earnings ratio as a determinant of the cost of equity. If a company has a price/earnings ratio of $20 to $1, rather than $10 to $1, does this really mean that its cost of equity capital is 5% rather than 10%? While mathematically this would seem so, in practice it would leave a company with a cost of capital hurdle rate so low as to make almost any investment acceptable. In a situation such as this one, a company's historical as well as its anticipated rate of earnings growth undoubtedly influence the price/earnings ratio it commands in the market. To take this factor into account, the approximate annual growth factor in excess of the industry average is added to the company's cost of equity. In our illustration, the company's basic cost of equity would thus be 5%.

$$\text{Cost of equity} = \frac{\text{earnings (\$1)}}{\text{price per share (\$20)}} = 5\%$$

If we assume that the company's earnings have grown at an annual compound rate of 18% compared to an industry average of 9%, then this differential of 9% would also be added to the basic cost of equity, giving a total cost of 14%.

Exactly how precise is this determination of the cost of capital using the variations discussed here? That is highly questionable, although it undoubtedly provides a more realistic hurdle rate than would be obtained with only the basic calculation. And now, having covered the crucial process of setting the rate of return, we conclude this review of the methods and procedures for the analysis of new capital investments and turn to a discussion of ROI concepts as a measure of overall business performance.

14

Fundamentals of Investment Analysis: Measuring Overall Business Performance Using ROI

In the preceding chapters we've discussed the importance of the return on new capital investments and the methods used to measure that return. ROI, as we have noted, also provides a reliable measure of overall business performance. In fact, many consider ROI to be the only meaningful measure of a company's success.

In this chapter we discuss how ROI is used to measure overall performance. First, a reminder: a company's performance reflects the success with which management chooses and executes new investments and the skill with which management handles old investments.

Return on overall business performance can usually be measured in three basic ways:

1. Return on shareholders' equity
2. Return on total investment
3. Return on total assets

The ratios used to calculate the overall rate of return on business investment in each of these three methods are derived from

Exhibit 14-1. Balance sheet, EZ Corporation, December 31, 19X2.

	19X1	19X2		19X1	19X2
Current assets	$180	$190	Current liabilities	$ 90	$100
Net fixed assets	80	103	Bonds payable	70	70
Other assets	10	10	Shareholders' equity	110	133
Total assets	$270	$303	Total liab. and equity	$270	$303

the balance sheet and the income statement, both of which are included in a company's annual statement. Simplified examples of the two schedules are shown in Exhibits 14-1 and 14-2.

Let's turn now to a detailed discussion of the three analytical methods and examine their uses and limitations.

Return on Shareholders' Equity

The most frequently used measure of return on investment is **return on shareholders' equity,** or return on shareholders' invest-

Exhibit 14-2. Income statement, EZ Corporation, for the period ending December 31, 19X2.

Sales	$400,000
Less cost of goods sold	280,000
Gross profit	$120,000
Less selling expenses	50,000
Less administrative expenses	20,000
Operating income	$ 50,000
Less interest expense	4,200
Income before taxes	$ 45,800
Less income taxes	22,800
Net income after taxes	$ 23,000

ment. The numerator of this ratio is the net income of the company for the period; the denominator is the shareholders' investment at the end of the period. So, for EZ Corporation, we have:

$$\frac{\text{Net income after taxes}}{\text{Shareholders' equity at year-end}} = \frac{\$\,23{,}000}{\$133{,}000} = 17.3\%$$

Although the ratio for the return on shareholders' equity always consists of net income as the numerator and shareholders' investment as the denominator, the ratio can be varied by adjusting either the numerator or the denominator. In most cases the denominator changes. For example, the net income for the period can be related to shareholders' investment at the beginning of the period rather than at the end. For EZ we would then have:

$$\frac{\text{Net income}}{\text{Shareholders' equity at beginning of year}} = \frac{\$\,23{,}000}{\$110{,}000} = 20.9\%$$

Another variation involves averaging the shareholders' investment at the beginning and at the end of the period. This variation gives the following return:

Shareholders' equity at beginning of year	$110,000
Shareholders' equity at end of year	133,000
	243,000 ÷ 2 = $121,500
Average shareholders' equity during year	121,500

$$\frac{\text{Net income}}{\text{Average shareholders' equity during year}} = \frac{\$23{,}000}{\$121{,}500} = 18.9\%$$

None of these variations is necessarily more correct than the others, although the last method given is the most frequently used. It does make sense; shareholders have a certain investment in the corporation at the beginning and at the end of the year; the average of the two figures represents the average investment on which earnings have been generated throughout the year. But what is important in ROI—as well as in any other analysis—and the point to be emphasized here is that one must know what approach has been used in any ROI calculation and that that ap-

Exhibit 14-3. Net income related to shareholders' equity and shareholders' original investment.

Net Income Related to Shareholders' Equity

Shareholders' original investment	$1,000,000
Retained earnings (losses)	(200,000)
Shareholders' equity	800,000
Net income for period	80,000

$$\frac{\text{Net income for period}}{\text{Shareholders' equity}} = \frac{80,000}{800,000} = 10\%$$

Return on shareholders' equity = 10%

Net Income Related to Shareholders' Original Investment

Net income for period	$ 80,000
Shareholders' original investment	1,000,000

Return on shareholders' original investment = 8%

proach has been used consistently throughout any period included in an analysis.

In its most common form, shareholders' equity includes the shareholders' original investment plus those earnings of the corporation that have been retained for internal expansion rather than paid out to shareholders as dividends. The corporation may incur losses rather than show earnings, however, and these losses also form part of shareholders' equity. Thus, shareholders' equity reflects any loss incurred by the corporation—that is, the shareholders' original investment is reduced by the corporation's accumulated losses.

In order to provide a meaningful calculation of the return on the shareholders' equity when a company experiences losses, the net income should be related to the shareholders' original investment rather than to shareholders' equity. Exhibit 14-3 shows the different results obtained when net income is related to shareholders' equity and when it is related to shareholders' original investment.

As its name suggests, the return on shareholders' equity quantifies the return on investment that the shareholders receive over a specified period of time. But the ratio is also a significant measure of how well the shareholders (through their elected board of directors) have managed the overall business and of how intelligently and how profitably management has used its custodianship.

For these reasons, return on shareholders' equity (as well as other return calculations that we will discuss later in this chapter) forms a key part of any objective evaluation of the current and prospective profitability and financial position of any business. Such evaluations are prepared by the services such as Standard & Poor's and Moody's and by leading financial publications such as *Fortune* and *Forbes*.

We should note that the return to the shareholder indicated by the ratio does not necessarily mean that the shareholder will receive that amount in cash. Corporate shareholders receive the cash return from their investment in the form of dividends. Although it is conceivable that a corporation might distribute 100% of each year's annual earnings as dividends, this is highly unlikely; some portion is usually retained in the business to finance further growth. We should also note that the investment included in the ratio is that of an original shareholder—the shareholder who subscribed to the stock of the corporation when it was originally issued. If the company has enjoyed some success, in all likelihood new shareholders will have paid a premium for their stock investments, and the return they enjoy will be the net income they receive in relation to the price they paid for the stock, not the original subscription price.

Finally, we should reemphasize the significance of return ratios in light of the accelerated and sometimes double-digit inflation that has been experienced at one time or another by most of the industrialized nations of the world. If a company fails to generate an ROI that is at least equal to the annual rate of inflation in the economy in which it has primary operations, the company is being decapitalized.

Return on Total Investment

The second method for determining return on investment is to calculate return on total capital. In this ratio the numerator is once

Exhibit 14-4. Return on total capital employed.

Net income after tax		$ 23,000
Add back interest on long-term debt		
Interest before tax	4,200	
Less tax deduction on interest expense at 48%	2,100	
Interest expense after tax		2,100
Net income after tax adjusted for interest		$ 25,100
Total Capital		
Long-term debt		$ 70,000
Shareholders' equity		133,000
		$203,000

$$\frac{\text{Net income + interest after tax}}{\text{Total capital}} = \frac{\$\ 25,100}{\$203,000} = 12.4\%$$

again the net income of the corporation for the appropriate period. The denominator, however, includes long-term permanent capital—funds borrowed for more than one year—in addition to shareholders' equity.

As shown in Exhibit 14-4, the first stage of calculating the return on total investment involves adjusting net income for the effect of the interest paid on the long-term capital. To do this, we simply add the interest on long-term debt to the net income after tax. We know from EZ's income statement (Exhibit 14-2) that the annual interest cost on long-term debt was $4,200. But here we have a problem. The interest cost of $4,200 was determined before income taxes and must be adjusted if it is to be added to income items that are on an after-tax basis. This can be done easily by multiplying the interest cost by the tax factor (48%, for example) and subtracting that amount from the interest cost. As we see from Exhibit 14-4, the net income after tax plus interest adjusted for taxes amounts to $25,100.

As we mentioned before, the denominator consists of shareholders' equity plus the long-term debt of the corporation. For EZ Corporation, the denominator is $203,000 ($70,000 of long-term debt plus $133,000 of shareholders' equity). EZ Corporation's return on total investment is 12.4%.

Exhibit 14-5. Comparative ROIs: EZ Corporation vs. competitor.

	EZ Corporation	Competitor
Long-term debt	$ 70,000	$100,000
Shareholders' equity	133,000	103,000
Total capital	$203,000	$203,000
Net income	$ 23,000	$ 22,100
Annual interest expense	4,200	6,000
Annual interest expense adjusted for taxes at 50%	2,100	3,000

Calculation of Return on Shareholders' Investment

Reported net income	$ 23,000	$ 22,100
	$133,000	$103,000
Percent equity on shareholders equity	17.3%	21.5%

The return on total capital is valuable because it indicates the return earned on all long-term sources of funds employed in the business, not only shareholders' investments. This ratio almost always accompanies the more basic and conventional return on shareholders' investment. If we look at Exhibit 14-5, we can better appreciate why.

Exhibit 14-5 compares the financial information presented for EZ Corporation in Exhibits 14-1 and 14-2 with that for a competitor. The competitor appears to be considerably more successful. It has a higher return on shareholders' investment (21.5% compared to 17.3% for EZ). But, as we show in Exhibit 14-6, both companies enjoy exactly the same return on total capital. The difference between the two companies is not that one earns a higher return on its investments than the other but that each has structured its permanent capital differently. Specifically, the competitor has a higher proportion of long-term debt as part of its total capital than does the EZ Corporation. In the jargon of the financial community, the competitor is said to be more **leveraged,** which may or may not be to its advantage. Nevertheless, the analysis

Exhibit 14-6. Comparative returns on total capital: EZ Corporation vs. competitor.

	EZ Corporation	Competitor
Reported net income	$ 23,000	$ 22,100
Add back annual interest expense adjusted for taxes	2,100	3,000
Totals	$ 25,100	$ 25,100

Calculation of Return on Total Capital

	EZ Corporation	Competitor
$\dfrac{\text{Reported net income adjusted for interest expense}}{\text{Total Capital}} =$	$\dfrac{\$\ 25,100}{\$203,000}$	$\dfrac{\$\ 25,100}{\$203,000}$
Percent return on total capital	12.4%	12.4%

of the return on total capital isolates the contribution of a major proportion of *long-term debt* to the appearance of higher profitability.

It should be noted that the return on total investment can be varied in the same ways as can the return on shareholders' equity; it can be based on total capital at both the beginning and end of the period and on the average total capital for the year.

Return on Total Assets

As its name suggests, the return on total assets calculation relates net income to all assets of the company. Thus, all items on the left side of the company's balance sheet are included in the denominator.

There are those who insist that return on total assets is the best measure of return because the other return calculations do not take short-term financing into account. They claim that short-term financing strongly influences the return calculation. By calculating return on total assets, no such distortion is possible because debt is not considered at all. For an example, let's take another look at the EZ Corporation. Once again we must adjust net income

Exhibit 14-7. Return on total assets.

Net income after taxes	$23,000
Plus interest expense after income taxes	2,100
Net income adjusted for interest after taxes	$25,100

$$\frac{\text{Adjusted net income}}{\text{Total assets}} = \frac{\$\ 25,000}{\$303,000} = 8.3\% \text{ return on total assets}$$

to reflect after-tax interest expense, so once again the numerator consists of net income plus interest expense adjusted for taxes, a total of $25,100. The denominator is the total assets of the EZ Corporation—$303,000. The return on total assets is 8.3%, as shown in Exhibit 14-7.

Return on total assets is lower than return on total investment because once again the investment denominator has increased at a much greater rate than the profit numerator.

Some General Considerations

Although we have confined our discussion of return on investment to its function as a measure of overall business performance, we should note that ROI is used extensively within corporate organizations as a managerial tool and as a yardstick of managerial performance.

Later in this chapter we provide a more detailed discussion of the internal applications of ROI analytical techniques. But for now we must recognize that ROI is often used as a technique for the evaluation not only of the value of business but also of managerial performance. These evaluations can be made under any one of the ROI analytical techniques that we have discussed. Interestingly enough, they may come up with results that appear to contradict the facts. For example, the return on a particular ROI center may be nominal—say, 4% to 6% a year. In the face of more attractive investment alternatives and even the going cost of short-term money at 9% a year, top management might well conclude that it should disinvest that center. But if the return on that center in earlier periods had been lower, or even nonexistent, a return of 4% might be an indication that the manager responsible for that center had in fact done an excellent job in the face of a difficult situation with limited potential.

As we have seen, return on investment calculations can be made in a variety of circumstances and with various approaches. For the nonfinancial executive, perhaps this fact, more than any other, is the most important thing to bear in mine.

But now let's look at some specific application and variations of ROI performance measures as they are used in many large complex organizations.

ROI Control Centers

The most basic and common application of the return on investment concept is the ROI control center. The growth, size, and complexity of the modern business organization have led to decentralization, with the responsibility and authority for the profitable operation of commercial activities delegated to small, manageable components of the enterprise. Organizational and accounting controls are developed to evaluate how effectively the manager of each of these components carries out his or her responsibilities.

These components, called **responsibility centers,** take several forms, one of the most basic of which is the **revenue center.** A segment of the organization is given responsibility for generating revenues to meet a specified target. The sales department of almost any organization is a good example of a revenue center; the revenue targets are the salesperson's dreaded annual sales "commitments."

The second kind of responsibility center, used at least as much as the revenue center, if not more so, is the **cost center.** A segment of the organization is given responsibility for controlling costs of operations over which it has authority. Almost all private and public organizations now use cost centers.

Although revenue and cost centers are useful in decentralization, they have obvious limitations. A revenue center isolates the responsibility for the generation of revenues but does not indicate the costs incurred to obtain the revenues; a cost center facilitates the control of costs but does not measure the revenues generated as a result of the costs incurred. Some typical examples of cost centers are a controller's office or a legal department.

The critical failure of the revenue and cost centers to match revenues against costs led to the development of the **profit center.** Profit-center management is responsible both for generating revenues and for controlling costs associated with those revenues.

Most large corporations and organizations today have profit centers for obvious reasons: the profit center focuses on a basic business objective—profitability. But despite the advantages of the profit center concept, it has one major defect: it does not take into account the fact that profits are relative. Let's look at two profit centers. Profit Center A earns $200,000 a year, whereas Profit Center B earns $400,000 a year.

	Profit Center A	*Profit Center B*
Net income	$ 200,000	$ 400,000
Investment	$1,000,000	$2,000,000
Return on investment	20%	20%

Profit Center B appears to be more profitable by far, but we know that any assessment based only on this information is premature and very possibly erroneous, since we have ignored a critical consideration—what funds have been invested to generate these profits.

Using these examples, we can see that if the investment is $1 million in Profit Center A and $2 million in Profit Center B, then the two centers are equally successful because they are both earning a 20% return on their investment.

The necessity of clarifying the relationship between profit and the investment used in generating that profit has led to the application of ROI to the responsibility concept. And so we have the final and most sophisticated form of the responsibility center—the ROI control center.

Managers of ROI control centers are delegated responsibility not only for the profitability of an operation but also for the most efficient use of the assets they control and that are used to generate that profit. The ROI center approach gives managers the incentive to deploy their capital intelligently. We have already learned how important having an objective is to the overall performance of the corporation.

The Residual Income Concept

Practically everybody agrees on the importance of adequate return on investment, but not everybody agrees that the ROI-center approach is the best method for measuring ROI. As we have seen, return on investment is derived from the relationship between profits and investment, and it's precisely this aspect that critics find objectionable. They argue that ROI is an index and that ROI tempts management merely to maximize the index rather than to maximize the *absolute* profits in relation to the capital employed.

One can more readily appreciate this point in the context of a personal investment situation. Would you, ask the critics, rather have a $10,000 investment yielding a 20% return or a $200,000 investment yielding a 12% return? The ready answer, for most of us, is that we would choose the greater investment income over the dramatically higher rate of return. But, say the critics, the conventional application of the ROI formula would encourage you to choose the investment with the higher return even though the actual amount of income would be less.

Out of concerns and criticisms such as these has come an adaptation of the ROI center approach called the **residual income** concept. Let's explore this concept by first looking at a comparison of two ROI centers based on the application for the standard ROI concepts.

In the conventional ROI calculation shown, ROI Center A appears to be more successful than ROI Center B. Critics of ROI, however, would argue that Center A merely has a higher index.

	Business A	*Business B*
Investment base	$1,000	$5,000
Net income	200	750
ROI	20%	15%

The real question, they would say, is whether it is better to earn a high rate of return on a small amount of capital or a modest rate of return on a larger amount of capital. To evaluate the performance of the two centers from this perspective, each center should be charged with its cost of capital. This cost is deducted from the stated profit of the center to arrive at the **residual income**—the income that remains after the cost of capital has been deducted. If we assume, for example, that the cost of capital applicable to the investments in both ROI Centers A and B is 12%, their comparative performance is as follows:

Net income	$200	$750
Less cost of capital	120	600
Residual income	$ 80	$150

Under the residual income concept, ROI Center B makes a greater absolute contribution to profits, even though it has the lower ROI ratio. Proponents of the residual income concept argue that this is a more relevant measure of performance than the rate of return and that the residual income concept provides a tool for the internal evaluation of managerial performance because:

1. It allows management to set absolute goals or standards for performance rather than merely to define an index of performance.

2. Different costs of capital can be applied to different segments of the business. The cost of capital applied to each segment reflects the degree of risk and the age of assets employed, thereby providing a more accurate assessment of the cost of capital than can be achieved by applying an overall rate.

3. When it is appropriate to do so, the same cost of capital can be applied to all assets, thereby allowing a direct comparison between profit performance of different ROI centers.

All of these advantages suggest that the residual income concept is preferable to the conventional ROI approach to managerial control and evaluation.

But the residual income concept is not without problems. Suppose, for example, that the cost of capital used in our previous illustrations is now 18% instead of 12%. The residual income of each operation then becomes:

Net income	$200	$750
Less cost of capital	180	900
Residual income	$ 20	$(150)

As we can see, the residual income concept cannot automatically point to the more successful ROI centers. The choice of the rate of return earned on the capital employed is obviously of overriding importance. Indeed, an objective evaluation of residual income performance can only be as meaningful only as the choice of the rate of return applied to the capital employed. On the other hand, it can be argued that even though residual income profitability at different costs of capital may vary, the cost of capital (and, hence, of true profitability) is totally obscured under the standard ROI approach. Thus, control systems based on the ROI concept can be used as an aid to, but never as a substitute for, good common-sense judgment. Nevertheless, ROI systems have—and will continue to have—significant influence on organization design and control.

Components of ROI

Although ROI is expressed as a single percentage, we can see from Exhibit 14-8 that it encompasses all the elements that go together to make up the profitability of a business organization. The comprehensiveness of the ROI calculation is a significant factor.

We can further note that return on investment calculation is the result of the interplay between two important aspects of the business: the rate of profit earned on sales (net profit ÷ sales) and the rate at which the assets employed in the business are "turned over" (sales ÷ investment). Generally speaking, profit-

Exhibit 14-8. Relationship of ROI to all the elements of profitability.

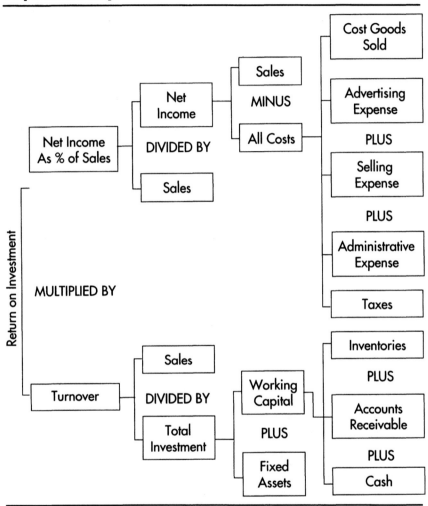

ability depends on sound control of costs and on adequate pricing as well as on successful selling. Turnover depends on the effective use of assets—both working capital and fixed investments—that are used to generate sales.

Businesses use different combinations of profit and turnover

Exhibit 14-9. ROI components.

	Company A Fast Pennies	Company B Slow Nickels
Sales	$5,000,000	$5,000,000
Net income	50,000	250,000
Investment	$500,000	$2,500,000
Net income as % sales	1%	5%
Investment turnover	10	2
ROI	1% × 10 = 10%	2% × 5 = 10%

ratios to generate an adequate return on their investments (see Exhibit 14-9). Business A and Business B enjoy exactly the same return but achieve it in dramatically different ways.

The turnover-to-profitability relationship provides a useful concept for incisive ROI analysis evaluation of ROI performance.

Other ROI Applications

Although ROI analysis has found its greatest use in the measurement of overall corporate and ROI control center performance, other applications of this important management tool are almost unlimited. Take, for example, the not uncommon business proposal for a sales-force expansion into two new districts. Assume that the estimated increases in sales and in operating profits for such an expansion are as shown in Exhibit 14-10. On the basis of

Exhibit 14-10. ROI analysis of district market expansion.

	Atlanta	Cleveland
Expected increase in:		
Sales	$100,000	$100,000
Cost of goods sold	55,000	55,000
Gross margin	45,000	45,000
Marketing costs	15,000	15,000
Operating profit	$30,000	$30,000

these figures, it appears that the district market expansion into Atlanta would produce the same results as expansion into Cleveland.

But you might also not that the all-important consideration—what investment must be made to support these expansions—has been ignored. Many make the mistake of assuming that because this is only a marketing expansion, no investment is involved. Nothing could be further from the truth. Investments are often thought of only in terms of additions to property, plant, and equipment, but in fact the "working capital" used to support a sales effort is a permanent investment. Working capital includes the accounts receivable (the credit that must nearly always be given to customers) and the product inventories that must be maintained to service purchase requests promptly.

Keep in mind that the investment in property, plant, and equipment is recovered not only through the earnings of the facility but also through the annual depreciation charges, which are not actual cash charges. In contrast, the investments that must be made to maintain the receivables and inventories are permanent investments and can be reduced only by means of absolute decreases in the amounts of accounts receivable inventory levels outstanding at any one time. So any marketing effort requires an investment of working capital, as is shown in Exhibit 14-11.

We can see that once the working capital investment required to support the market expansions is identified (assuming, of course, that the estimates are reasonable), Cleveland is found to be a more attractive location than Atlanta. By using the turnover-to-profitability approach to ROI analysis, we can see that the higher return in Cleveland is the result of more frequent turnover of assets than is anticipated for Atlanta.

The ROI approach can be used not only to analyze initial investment but also to monitor performance. The approach can therefore be used to evaluate the Cleveland district manager's performance—how well he or she meets sales objectives and controls marketing costs and how well he or she manages the accounts receivable and inventories used to generate these sales. Sales managers cannot simply emphasize "volume"; they must operate in an overall business context and attempt to optimize the return on investment.

Exhibit 14-11. More detailed ROI analysis of district market expansion.

	Atlanta	Cleveland
Expected increase in:		
Sales	$100,000	$100,000
Cost of goods sold	55,000	55,000
Gross margin	45,000	45,000
Marketing costs	15,000	15,000
Operating profit	$30,000	$30,000
Accounts receivable	17,000	25,000
Inventories	33,000	10,000
Total investment	$50,000	$35,000
Profit on sales	30%	30%
Investment turnover	2.0 times	2.9 times
Return on assets managed (ROAM)	60%	86%

The application of the return on investment concept to the sales/marketing function, which was illustrated here and in Exhibit 14-11, is often referred to as **ROAM**—return on assets managed—and is widely used.

Analysis of ROI by Product

An additional and even more probing application of ROI analysis is the analysis of ROI by individual product. Since the mid-1980s, both theoreticians and practitioners of cost accounting have placed increased emphasis on the identification of **product profitability.** A detailed discussion of the methods and the complexities of this application of ROI are beyond our purpose here. But the point is that it can be done. Exhibit 14-12 shows what a typical product profit statement might look like under the "contribution concept" or "product profitability."

As important as profitability by product may be, even more meaningful is the return on investment by product. Even though it is difficult to identify ROI by product, it is by no means impossible. For example, we have pointed out that any product requires

Exhibit 14-12. Analysis of ROI by products, EZ Corporation.

	Product X	Product Y	Product Z	Total
Sales	$230,000	$125,000	$42,000	$397,000
Less variable costs				
Production	125,000	70,000	20,000	215,000
Marketing— commissions	15,000	6,000	2,000	23,000
Marketing— transportation	7,000	2,400	500	9,900
Total variable costs	$147,000	$ 78,400	$22,500	$247,900
Contribution after variable costs	83,000	46,600	19,500	149,100
Less direct fixed costs				
Production	15,000	8,000	3,000	26,000
Marketing	10,000	8,000	3,000	21,000
Total direct fixed costs	25,000	16,000	6,000	47,000
Product contribution	$ 58,000	$ 30,600	$13,500	$102,100
Less indirect fixed expenses				
Manufacturing				20,000
Selling				20,000
Administrative				10,000
Total indirect fixed expenses				50,000
Operating profit				$ 52,100

a working capital investment in both receivables and inventories. In product ROI analysis, the level of receivables and of inventories associated with each product needs to be identified.

The next step is to identify the investment in plant and manufacturing facilities associated with the product. This analysis may present some difficulties. If a single product is manufactured in a single location and all the plant and equipment is used in manufacturing that product, then of course there will be no problem. Unfortunately, more often a variety of products is manufactured in the same factory and sometimes even on the same equipment.

Exhibit 14-13. More detailed ROI analysis by products, EZ Corporation.

	Product X	Product Y	Product Z	Total
Sales	$230,000	$125,000	$42,000	$397,000
Less variable costs				
Production	125,000	70,000	20,000	215,000
Marketing—				
commissions	15,000	6,000	2,000	23,000
Marketing—				
transportation	7,000	2,400	500	9,900
Total variable costs	$147,000	$ 78,400	$22,500	$247,900
Contribution after				
variable costs	83,000	46,600	19,500	149,100
Less direct fixed costs				
Production	15,000	8,000	3,000	26,000
Marketing	10,000	8,000	3,000	21,000
Total direct fixed costs	25,000	16,000	6,000	47,000
Product contribution	$ 58,000	$ 30,600	$13,500	$102,100
Less indirect				
fixed expenses				
Manufacturing				20,000
Selling				20,000
Administrative				10,000
Total indirect fixed				
expenses				50,000
Operating profit				$ 52,100
Investment by Product				
Receivables	46,000	25,000	5,000	76,000
Inventories	40,000	20,000	10,000	70,000
Direct production				
investment	150,000	40,000	60,000	250,000
Indirect production				
investment	40,000	30,000	30,000	100,000
Total investment	276,000	115,000	105,000	496,000
% Return product				
contribution to				
investment	21.0	26.6	12.9	20.5
% Return total group				
operating profit to				
investment	—	—	—	10.5

When this is the case, the analyst is faced with the problem of allocating portions of the investment to each individual product.

Again, it is not within the scope of this book to present a detailed discussion of such an effort; it suffices to say that such an allocation *is* possible. The accuracy of the allocation can always be disputed, but isn't it better to attempt an analysis than to ignore it totally? Exhibit 14-13 shows what an ROI analysis of the products used in our preceding example might look like.

From this exhibit, it is evident that the product that first appears most desirable may not be so when we have identified the associated investments. For example, whereas Product X appears to have the highest profitability (product contribution), Product Y is in fact the most successful on an ROI basis (26.6%).

Much has been written about the problems and challenges that face the manager of private business in the future. There is universal agreement that the increasing scarcity of capital is one of the most significant of these challenges. Basic ROI analysis—along with its many applications and variations—will continue to be an important tool in the analysis and evaluation of business's efforts to use this increasingly scarce resource to its fullest.

15

Fundamentals of Financial Analysis: Balance Sheets and Income Statements

To begin, let us assume nothing and ask the basic question: Why financial analysis? The following earnings results were obtained by one company in 1995:

Earnings per share		55 cents
Sales	$33,667,319	
Net income	$859,523	

This information is not extensive, but it does include the key data from an income statement. Still, it's hard to draw a conclusion. Is the fact that the corporation earned 55 cents per share in 1995 good or bad? We need to stop and ask, what are the basic objectives of the business?

As we have stressed in the preceding chapters, one of the most basic and perhaps most important objectives of any business is to earn a satisfactory return on investment. One of the major purposes of financial analysis is to measure the success a business has in achieving this goal. In Chapter 14 we discussed the several ways that ROI investment/financial analysis is used to measure overall business performance.

Although adequacy of return on invested funds is the sine qua non of business endeavor, there are of course other considerations; a sound financial position and adequate levels of profitability must be maintained.

In this chapter, we focus on financial analysis techniques that facilitate the measurement and evaluation of a business's progress in maintaining both a satisfactory financial position and an adequate level of profitability.

Assessing Financial Condition

The maintenance of a satisfactory financial condition usually has two components—short-term financial position and adequate long-term position—or, to describe it differently, adequate liquidity and adequate solvency. **Liquidity** is the ability of a business to meet its short-term financial obligations promptly and satisfactorily; **solvency** is its ability to meet its longer-term financial obligations.

The techniques of financial analysis can be broken down into logical groups that measure and evaluate these two components—liquidity and solvency—along with a third corporate profitability.

Ratios are the primary method of financial analysis. A ratio is simply the mathematical relationship of one number to another. Percentages are the expression of a ratio when the base is 100. Let's look now at some specific applications of ratios and percentages in the three areas of financial analysis that we have discussed. We will use the financial data that appear in the balance sheet and the income statement of XYZ Too Machinery, Inc., as shown in Exhibit 15-1.

Liquidity Analysis

Liquidity is the ability of a corporation to meet its current obligations out of its current assets. These assets appear as the first major category on the left side of the balance sheet. Assets are ranked in order of their liquidity, beginning with cash. On the

Exhibit 15-1. Balance sheet and income statement for XYZ Tool Machinery, Inc.

Balance Sheet
($000)
December 31, 19X5

	19X4	19X5		19X4	19X5
Current assets			Current liabilities		
Cash	$ 40	$ 50	Accounts payable	$ 40	$ 50
Accounts receivable—Net	50	60	Accrued wages	20	30
Inventory	70	60	Accrued taxes	30	20
Prepaid expenses	20	20	Total current liabilities	$ 90	$100
Total current assets	$180	$190			
Fixed assets			*Long-term liabilities*		
Property, plant, and equipment	$150	$183	Bonds payable	70	70
Less accumulated depreciation	70	80	Total long-term liabilities	$ 70	$ 70

Net property, plant, and equipment	80		
Total fixed assets	$ 80	103	$103
Other assets	10	10	
Total assets	$270	$303	$303

Shareholders' equity			
Common stock	60		60
Retained earnings	50		73
Total shareholders' equity		$110	$133
Total equities		$270	$303

Income Statement
For Period Ending 19X5

Net Sales	$400,000
Less cost of sales	280,000
Gross profit	$120,000
Less selling expenses	50,000
Less administrative expenses	20,000
Operating income	$ 50,000
Interest expense	4,200
Income before taxes	$ 45,800
Income taxes	22,800
Net income	$23,000

right side of the balance sheet the converse of current assets—liabilities—is shown, usually in order of the immediacy of payment.

Current assets are, by definition, either cash or other assets that will be converted to cash in the course of a year. Current liabilities are those that are due and payable within a year. Under normal circumstances, a business uses its current assets to pay its current liabilities, since both of them are involved in an annual receivable payment cycle.

Current Ratio

The first ratio, and one of the most commonly used, for measuring the relationship of assets to liabilities is the **current ratio.** It is obtained by dividing the current assets of a business by its current liabilities and is calculated from the 19X5 figures for XYZ Tool Machinery, Inc.'s balance sheet in Exhibit 15-1 as follows:

$$\frac{\text{Current assets}}{\text{Current liabilities}} = \frac{\$190,000}{\$100,000} = 1.9 \text{ current ratio}$$

We can interpret the current ratio of the company as follows: It has $1.90 of current assets to meet $1 of debt due as a current liability.

In using ratios for financial analysis, each individual situation must be considered. However, as a general rule, a current ratio of 2:1 is considered to be quite healthy in American business practices.

Quick Ratio

Current assets usually include three basic items—cash, accounts receivable, and inventories. When we evaluate the liquidity of a company on the basis of its current ratio, we assume that the inventory that figures as part of the total current assets is liquid. This assumption, however, may not always be realistic. For example, obsolete merchandise may appear as an item of inventory but in fact have no value whatsoever. In the same way, inventory may be represented by several large items, such as a boat in the case of a marina, that may not necessarily become liquid in a short period of time.

For this reason, a second and more stringent evaluation of a company's liquidity can be obtained by the so-called **quick ratio**, sometimes called the **acid test ratio**. The quick ratio is computed by taking the "quick" assets of a corporation, which are defined as cash and accounts receivable-net, and relating them to the total current liabilities of the corporation. Using the figures from XYZ Tool Machinery's Balance Sheet, the quick ratio is:

Cash	$ 50,000	
Accounts receivable net	60,000	$110,000 = 1.1 quick ratio
Quick assets	$110,000	$100,000
Current liabilities	$100,000	

The company has a quick ratio of 1.1 to 1. That is, there is $1.10 of quick assets that can be used to meet the payments of current liabilities. The results of this particular quick ratio indicate that if the company were really pressed and not able to sell quickly the merchandise that it holds in inventory, it would still be able to meet all its current obligations out of both its cash and accounts receivable. As a rule of thumb, a quick ratio of 1.1 to 1 is generally considered adequate. Once again, however, we need to be careful in making generalizations, since the unique aspects of each individual situation surrounding a particular company's business must be considered.

Although the quick or acid test ratio subjects the company to a much more rigorous evaluation of its liquidity, the quick assets include the accounts receivable of the business. The ratio therefore implicitly assumes that the accounts receivable-net are readily collectible and in fact have liquidity. Under normal conditions, we would expect this to be the case.

We can, however, specifically evaluate the collectibility of a business's accounts receivable-net by determining the relationship of receivables to the total annual sales. The receivable data are available from the balance sheet and the annual sales data appear on the income statement.

Average Collection Period

The numbers from XYZ Tool Machinery indicate that account receivables-net at year end 19X5 of $60,000 are 15% of the total annual sales of $400,000 for the company in 19X5. Total sales for the company were made over the period of a year, or 365 days. If the accounts receivable-net represent 15% of annual sales in terms of dollars, they also represent 15% of the 365 days over which they were made. Fifteen percent of 365 days equals 55 days (rounded). This means that, on average, the company takes 55 days to collect its accounts receivable-net. On an individual basis, some of these accounts receivable-net may be collected in a shorter period of time and others in a longer period of time. On average, however, 55 calendar days pass before an account receivable is collected and becomes cash. This is often referred to as the **average collection period.**

The calculation of this period helps evaluate the liquidity of a company's accounts receivable-net. If the results for XYZ Tool Machinery resulted in an average collection period of 180 days, we would, of course, have a different assessment of the speed with which the accounts receivable could be liquidated to obtain cash for the payment of current liabilities.

Determination of what's par in terms of an average collection for a company is somewhat difficult. Collection times fluctuate depending on the credit terms, that is, on the amount of time the company allows its customers to pay their bills. If, for example, a company allows 60 days of credit outstanding, then its average collection period will equal 60 days. If, however, as is so commonly the case, 30 days of credit is the normal period of time extended, then anything over 30 days represents a collection period beyond established credit terms. As a practical matter, not all customers pay their bills promptly, so there is always some excess over the formal credit terms extended by the company. If a company is generous in its extension of credit terms, more funds will be required and the liquidity of its receivables will be reduced. The calculation of days sales outstanding can be and often is refined by making use of monthly sales data; the credit sales for the preceding months are added until they reach the amount shown as receivables. For example:

Accounts receivable-net, December 31, 19X5 = $60,000			
Credit Sales ($000)			
December	November	October	September
25	15	20	30

Accounts receivable-net must include all of December's sales plus November's sales plus the $20,000 sold in October. This means that days outstanding, or the collection period, is shown as follows:

Month	Amount	Days
December	All	31
November	All	30
October	All	31
		92

The foregoing approach provides a more accurate assessment and is particularly useful in businesses that have a seasonal sales pattern.

Inventory Turnover Ratio

The quick or acid test ratio recognizes the potential liquidity problems in inventories but does nothing to analyze them. It simply ignores them. As a practical matter, the liquidity of a company's inventories can be even more important than the liquidity of receivables. To assess this, the analyst makes use of the **inventory turnover ratio,** which is very similar to the average collection period. It is calculated by using the cost of sales from the income statement divided by the average inventory (which is obtained from data on this item from the balance sheet). The inventory turnover ratio for XYZ Tool Machinery is calculated in the following manner:

$$\frac{\text{Cost of sales for 1995}}{\text{Average inventory year end 1994 and 1995}} = \frac{\$280,000}{(70,000 + 60,000)/2}$$

$$= \frac{\$280,000}{65,000} = 4.3$$

By dividing the average inventory into the cost of sales, we obtain a ratio of 4.3. To interpret this ratio, we employ the same logic that we used in determining the average collection period. If the cost of sales is the total cost incurred over a period of one year, 19X5, and the average of the inventory at the end of 19X4 and 19X5 is $65,000, this means that the inventory "turned over" 4.3 times during the year; that is, the company sold its inventory approximately one time every 85 days (365 days divided by 4.3), and its inventory of $65,000 can be converted to $65,000 of either accounts receivable-net or cash in a period of a little under three months.

By itself, the inventory turnover ratio indicates how long it takes a company to liquidate its inventories either into accounts receivable-net or into cash. Also, a business's inventory turnover ratios can be revealing when they are compared over a period of time. If over a particular period the inventory turnover ratio declines, that is, if it decreases from 4.3 to 4.0 to 3.5, this decrease suggests that the company's product is becoming less salable, portending difficulties for the company. In some situations, a decline in inventory turnover may simply reflect a general economic slowdown with reduced personal consumption.

Many additional ratios can be used to analyze the company's liquidity. The four we've reviewed, however, present the fundamentals. Let's turn next to the analysis of business solvency.

Solvency Analyses

The *Random House Dictionary of the English Language, 2nd ed.* (New York: Random House, 1987), defines solvency as the "ability to pay all just debts." Under this definition, liquidity and solvency appear to be much the same thing. As we indicated at the outset of this chapter, however, we are considering liquidity as the ability to maintain a sound financial position over the short term and solvency as the ability to maintain a sound financial position over a longer term.

This distinction is more than academic, for a company requires more than short-term capital. In the life of every company, there comes a point when it can no longer finance its operations on the basis of current liabilities. When this occurs, it can look either for long-term debt, involving repayment terms of anywhere from five to 25 years, or for additional shareholders' equity. Shareholders' equity, which in the case of a corporation involves the issuance of common (or preferred) stock, is almost always totally permanent capital. Long-term debt, on the other hand, must be repaid and also bears an interest cost that, along with the principal, must be paid by the business. For the purposes of most financial analyses, however, long-term debt can be considered relatively permanent capital. The most common form of long-term debt is bonds, which appear as long-term liabilities on the balance sheet, just above shareholder's equity.

The analysis of corporate solvency involves an examination of the adequacy of the permanent source of capital available to a business. The first and most common ratio used in this evaluation is the so-called debt-equity ratio.

Debt-Equity Ratio

The **debt-equity ratio** measures the amount of long-term debt in relation to the amount of shareholders' equity that a business has as its permanent capital. This is arrived at by adding the long-term debt and the shareholders' equity to find total permanent capital and then determining the percentage of each in relation to the total, yielding the debt-equity ratio. For XYZ Tool Machinery, this calculation is:

Long-term debt (liabilities)	$ 70,000
Shareholders' equity	133,000
Total	$203,000

$$\frac{\text{Long-term debt: } \$70,000}{\text{Long-term debt } + \text{ shareholders' equity: } \$203,000} = .35$$

The debt-equity ratio of .35 means that 35 cents of every one dollar of permanent capital is long-term debt. Put another way, the shareholders have invested approximately $2 for every $1 of long-term debt in the corporation. The interpretation of the debt-equity ratio obviously is a judgment call. If, however, the debt-equity ratio indicates that the long-term debtors of the company have invested more money than the shareholders, there may be cause for concern about the adequacy of the permanent capital available for the company.

A very rough rule of thumb in U.S. business is that a company's debt-equity ratio should not exceed .33. That is to say, it is assumed that over the long term a corporation cannot incur more than $1 of long-term debt for every $3 of permanent capital (long-term debt plus shareholders' equity). Many businesses, of course, do not operate within this particular capital structure. A business with a very high debt-equity ratio or a greater proportion of long-term debt is said to be undercapitalized.

Insufficient shareholders' equity, or undercapitalization, can have several adverse consequences. To ensure growth, a business must make new investments on a continuing basis. But since long-term debt requires repayment, the earnings that can be reinvested are not always sufficient for this purpose. Therefore, a company with insufficient shareholders' equity may have to restrain its growth.

There is a second way to calculate a debt-equity ratio. Our illustration took the relationship of the long-term debt to the total of long-term debt and shareholders' equity. An alternate approach is to determine the proportionate relationship between the long-term debt (liabilities) and the equity capital. In the case of XYZ Tool Machinery, this would be $70,000 to $133,000, or a ratio of .53. This method gives a higher debt-equity ratio.

A clear understanding of the approach used to calculate the debt-equity ratio is imperative for the proper analysis and interpretation of the ratio. The conventional yardstick of a .33 ratio is based on the calculation using the sum of long-term debt (liabilities) and shareholders' equity as the denominator.

If a company obtains a disproportionate amount of its permanent capital in the form of long-term debt, it may become burdened with excessively large payments associated with the long-term debt. We examine this particular aspect by discussing another ratio associated with solvency, the times-interest-earned ratio.

Times-Interest-Earned Ratio

Long-term debt may be obtained from a private institution or on the bond market. Whatever the source, however, a fixed annual interest cost is attached to the use of the capital. As a general rule, when a corporation is unable to pay this annual fixed cost, the creditor has a right to demand payment not only of any interest due but also of the principal of the original sum he loaned. For this reason it becomes important for business to be able to meet its fixed annual interest obligations.

The ratio that attempts to qualify the company's ability to meet its debt payments is called the **times-interest-earned ratio,** which is calculated as follows. First, the operating income of the company is obtained from the income statement. Second, this figure is divided by the annual interest expense associated with the company's long-term debt to arrive at the times-interest-earned ratio.

The annual interest cost can usually be obtained from the income statement. In some cases, however, it may be necessary to separate the interest cost associated with short-term borrowing from that of long-term borrowing. The times-interest-earned ratio for XYZ Tool Machinery is calculated as follows:

$$\frac{\text{Operating income}}{\text{Interest expense on bonds}} = \frac{\$50,000}{\$4,200} = 11.9$$

From this calculation, we see that for the period ending 19X5 the operating profits of the company were 11.9 times greater than the annual amount of interest it was required to pay on their long-term debt. A very significant change in the level of the company's profitability would have to occur before the company's ability to meet its annual interest payment would be seriously jeopardized. If, for example, the times-interest-earned ratio had been only 1.2 or 1.5, we might have begun to worry whether the company could meet these fixed annual payments if the business were to be adversely affected by a slowdown in the economy or a dropoff in the sales of a major product.

A technical point here is that the times-interest-earned ratio takes the interest cost before, rather than after, taxes. This is done because the operating profits used in the numerator are profits before taxes, not after; to obtain a comparable relationship, the interest costs used in this calculation must also be on a before-tax basis.

Profitability Analysis

A corporation may be liquid and solvent. Unless it is profitable, however, its liquidity and solvency are probably not too significant. As we said earlier, profitability is the sine qua non of U.S. corporate enterprise. Let's now look at some of the analytical ratios that are used to evaluate profitability.

Net Profit as a Percentage of Sales

One of the most common ways to express corporate profitability is express net profit as a percentage of each dollar of sales. In this ratio, annual net income becomes the numerator of the equation, and the total annual net sales becomes the denominator. Net profits as a percentage of sales of XYZ Tool Machinery are calculated as follows:

$$\frac{\text{Net income}}{\text{Annual net sales}} = \frac{\$23,000}{\$400,000} = 5.8$$

This ratio tells us that the company makes a net profit of 5.8 cents on every dollar of sales.

Gross Margin

Another commonly used measure of profitability is the gross margin as a percentage of net sales. Gross margin results from the deduction of cost of sales from net sales. The calculation is exactly the same as that for relating net income to net sales except that gross profit is used as the numerator. The gross margin as a percent of net sales for XYZ is calculated as shown:

$$\frac{\text{Gross profit}}{\text{Annual net sales}} = \frac{\$120,000}{\$400,000} = 30\%$$

The gross margin ratio indicates how much the company has in terms of cents per sales dollar with which to cover the selling and administrative expenses of its operation.

The higher either gross or net profit as a percentage of net sales, the better. It is preferable for a company to achieve a net-income-to-net-sales ratio of 10 percent on every sales dollar rather than a ratio of 5 percent. Likewise, a gross margin of 45 percent is better than a gross margin of 35 percent.

Gross margin or net income ratios, like other financial ratios, become even more meaningful when they are used to evaluate profit results over a period of time. Thus, if an analysis of the past five years of net income as a percentage of net sales indicates that the ratio is declining, the business is experiencing a significant and perhaps ominous change. Likewise, a gross margin trend can be highly indicative; it may suggest either that raw material costs are increasing or that manufacturing efficiency is waning.

Gross margin and net income ratios certainly have their place in financial analysis, but they evaluate only profitability. We can't really get a proper perspective until we relate the profitability of venture to the funds that have been invested. For this evaluation, the financial analyst must turn to ratios that measure profits in relation to investment, as we discussed in Chapter 14.

Financial Analysis: Some Disclaimers

The techniques of financial analysis can be extremely effective instruments for incisive and meaningful interpretations of accounting data. They should always be used, however, with full appreciation of the limitations of the particular accounting data from which they are generated. These have been mentioned at various points in this book and are only touched on here:

- *Money Only.* Accounting measures business results only in terms of money. With this constraint, significant aspects of a business may be overlooked, both in the accounting records and in a financial analysis of them.
- *History.* The past may be prologue, but the chances of this being true in today's dynamic and changing business world are remote. Accounting data are historical. They track only where a business has been. Ratios derived from this history beg the really difficult question of where a business is going.
- *The Cost Concept.* Under the cost concept, most balance sheet values are at cost. Despite its advantages, this particular approach has limitations that grow even more pronounced as the rate of inflation increases. Accounting data, based on the cost concept, are in a certain sense unrealistic, and the ratios developed from them suffer the same deficiency.
- *Options.* Accounting is much more of an art than a science, at least in the sense that much is left to the discretion of the accountant. There are options, however, such as in the choice of LIFO, FIFO, or the Average Method; in methods of depreciation; in estimates of salvage value of fixed assets; and in manufacturing cost methods.

Financial ratios, and all other managerial tools, are an aid to—but not a substitute for—sound business judgment.

16

Understanding Cash Flows

There's a common saying on Wall Street that "cash is king." To understand why cash is useful, we can refer again to Robert Heller's book *The Great Executive Dream*, cited in Chapter 12, which describes the consequences of not having enough cash to operate a business: "Any small businessman who has had trouble meeting the payroll knows the painful principle: without enough cash, you drown." One aspect of the leveraged buyout and takeover frenzy of the late 1980s was the optimistic assessment of companies' cash flows and the amount of debt that they could service. It's no wonder that a company's cash flow statement has become such a vital and important part of its financial reporting package.

In this chapter we discuss the importance and the process of understanding cash flows and the role cash flow plays in keeping an organization healthy and prosperous.

Defining Cash Flows

In almost every organization, cash flows are generated from virtually every activity. Cash inflows and outflows are generated from different activities. To understand the movement of cash flows within a typical organization, it's important to understand which activities generate cash inflows and which generate outflows of cash.

Cash inflows are generated from any activity that adds to the cash balance of the organization, such as sales paid for in cash and sales that are collected from accounts receivable. Two other major sources of cash are the sale of securities that were held for investment purposes and monies borrowed from lenders to support expansion and growth activities.

On the opposite side are activities that create outflows of cash and that deduct from the cash balance of the organization. These include purchases of marketable securities, loan repayments to lenders, interest and principal payments to bondholders, payments to suppliers for merchandise purchased either for cash or as a payment of an existing accounts payable, payments to stockholders in the form of cash dividends, tax payments to government bodies, and payments to employees in the form of wages and benefits.

Decisions That Impact Cash Balances

During the course of operating a business, managers make some decisions that increase an organization's cash balance and some that result in decreases. To manage the organization effectively, the organization must balance cash increases and decreases in a way that provides adequate liquidity at all times. When there are more cash increases than cash decreases, the company can make temporary investments, usually in the form of marketable securities. When cash decreases exceed cash increases, it can turn to temporary short-term borrowings to provide temporary funding.

Decisions that can increase cash balances may involve reducing the amounts of accounts receivable, selling off both unproductive assets and obsolete inventory, deferring payments to creditors without jeopardizing the company's credit rating, acquiring both short- and long-term funds, and retaining more earnings within the business by generating higher profits.

Decisions that can decrease cash balances may involve extending more credit to customers (leading to higher accounts receivable), building up higher inventories, investing in more fixed assets, paying taxes and higher dividends, paying both short- and long-term borrowings, and retaining less earnings within the business by generating lower profits or losses.

Exhibit 16-1. Sample format for a statement of cash flows.

Company Name
Statement of Cash Flows
Time Period

Cash flows from operating activities		
(Details of cash inflows/outflows)	$XX	
Net cash (used in) provided by operating activities		$XX
Cash flows from investing activities		
(Details of cash inflows/outflows)	$XX	
Net cash (used in) investing activities		XX
Cash flows from financing activities		
(Details of cash inflows/outflows)	$XX	
Net cash provided by (used in) financing activities		$XX
Net increase (decrease) in cash		XX
Cash at beginning of year		XX
Cash at end of year		$XX

Statement of Cash Flows

To describe the movement of cash through various activities within an organization, accountants prepare a statement of cash flows as part of an organization's financial statements. The statement of cash flows provides information about cash receipts and payments and classifies them into three categories: cash flows generated from operating activities, cash flows generated from investing activities, and cash flows generated from financing activities for a specific period of time. When these three categories are combined, the resultant calculations explain and reconcile the net increase (decrease) in cash from the beginning of the period to the end of the period. Exhibit 16-1 illustrates the basic format that is used in preparing a statement of cash flows.

The statement of cash flows contains information on cash flow from three sources of income: operating activity, investing activity, and financing activity.

1. *Operating activities*. These are activities that include all transactions and events that are not classified as either investing or financing activities. They generate cash flows from an organization's operating activities, such as the selling of merchandise, or from services offered. They are broken down into the following cash inflows and outflows:

Cash inflows

- Cash receipts from customers for the sales of goods or services
- Collection or sale of accounts and short- and long-term notes receivable arising from these sales
- Cash receipts from return on loans (interest), other debt instruments, and dividends on equity securities
- Others not classified as investing or financing activities and events

Cash outflows

- Cash payments to suppliers for purchased inventory
- Cash payments to employees and other suppliers for goods or services
- Cash payments to government agencies for taxes due
- Cash payments of interest to lenders and other creditors

All other expenses are classified as operating activities. Most of this information comes from the income statement, current assets, and current liabilities.

2. *Investing activities*. These are activities that include lending and collecting on loans, buying and selling debt or equity investments, and acquiring and disposing of long-term fixed and intangible assets. Most of this information is found in the noncurrent asset section of the balance sheet. The cash outflows and inflows are as follows.

Cash inflows

- Cash receipts from the sales of fixed and intangible assets

- Cash receipts from the sales of debt or equity instruments of other companies
- Cash receipts from the collection or sales of other entities' debt instruments that were purchased by the company

Cash outflows

- Cash disbursements to purchase fixed and intangible assets
- Cash payments for the purchase of debt or equity instruments of other companies
- Disbursements of loans to other entities

3. *Financing activities.* These activities involve liability and owners' equity capital and result in a return on the owners' investments. They also include the acquisition of cash from creditors and the repayment of amounts borrowed. Information on financing activities is obtained from the liabilities and the equity sections of the balance sheet. Cash inflows and cash outflows are as follows.

Cash inflows

- Cash receipts from the sales of equity instruments, such as common and preferred stock
- The receipt of proceeds from the issuance of such debt instruments as bonds, notes, mortgages, and other short- and long-term borrowings

Cash outflows

- Dividend payments or other distributions to stockholders
- The acquisition or reacquisition of capital stock, such as treasury stock
- The repayment of long-term debt on outstanding bonds, mortgages, and other notes

Preparing the Statement of Cash Flows

There are two methods of preparing the statement of cash flows—the indirect method and the direct method. In both cases the cash flows that are presented must be converted from an accrual basis to a cash basis. Both of these methods arrive at the same results, but they differ in the disclosure of the items that make up the total amounts. Most companies prefer to use the indirect method, which we used in Exhibit 16-1. This method is easier to prepare and is sometimes referred to as the "reconciliation" method, since it reconciles net income to net cash flow from operations. The data also flow from financial data stored in the company's general ledger.

The direct method requires that the company present information in a way that is not done normally by converting operating cash revenues and expenses into a corresponding account. Both methods are illustrated in the following examples.

The Indirect Method

In order to convert net income to net cash flow from operating activities, it is necessary to make certain adjustments. These adjustments either add or deduct from net income and are summarized in the table.

Adjustment Explanations

In order to understand the reasons for these adjustments, you may find it helpful to review these explanations of the rationale behind them.

1. *Accounts receivable.* Decreases indicate that cash collections were greater than sales and therefore need to be added. Conversely, increases suggest that sales were greater than collections and that the difference needs to be deducted from sales since that difference was not collected in cash.

2. *Inventories.* Changes in inventories indicate whether more inventory was purchased than sold or vice versa. Increases must be added to cost of goods, whereas decreases must be deducted.

3. *Accounts payable.* This category indicates whether cash payments were greater or lower than what was actually purchased.

INDIRECT METHOD CONVERSION SCHEDULE

	Net Income	
	Add	*Deduct*
Depreciation/amortization	X	
Investing/financing losses	X	
Investing/financing gains		X
Accounts receivable—decrease	X	
Accounts receivable—increase		X
Inventory—decrease	X	
Inventory—increase		X
Prepaid expense—decrease	X	
Prepaid expense—increase		X
Accounts payable—increase	X	
Accounts payable—decrease		X
Accrued liabilities—increase	X	
Accrued liabilities—decrease		X
Interest payable—increase	X	
Interest payable—decrease		X
Income tax payable—increase	X	
Income tax payable—decrease		X

A decrease is added to cost of goods, whereas an increase is deducted.

4. *Prepaid expenses.* This figure reveals whether the monies paid for the prepayments exceeded or fell below the amount recorded as an expense. Increases are added to selling, general, and administrative expenses (operating or SG&A expenses), and decreases are deducted.

5. *Accrued liabilities/accounts payable.* This category reflects how much monies paid either exceeded or fell below the amount recorded as an expense. Decreases are added and increases deducted from SG&A expenses (operating expenses).

Exhibit 16-2. Sample income statement.

The Corporation
For the Year Ended December 31, 19X2

Sales	$180,000
Cost of sales	100,000
Gross profit	80,000
Selling, general and administrative expenses	29,000
Depreciation expense	6,500
Interest expense	5,000
Income before income taxes	39,500
Income taxes	10,500
Net income	$ 29,000

6. *Interest payable/taxes payable.* This amount indicates how much was paid that exceeded or fell below the interest/tax expense on the books. Decreases are added and increases deducted.

7. *Asset account changes.* Changes in asset accounts other than those used for computing cash flow from operating activities are considered investing activities. Increases in these accounts represent cash outflows and decreases represent cash inflows.

8. *Liability/stockholders' equity changes.* Changes in these accounts other than those used to compute cash flow from operating activities are considered financing activities.

Using Exhibits 16-2 and 16-3 as the basis for computation, Exhibit 16-4 illustrates how the statement of cash flows is prepared using the indirect method.

The Direct Method

The direct method requires converting both revenues and expenses to a corresponding cash account. This is accomplished by making the following adjustments from operating activities in order to convert these accounts into equivalent cash accounts.

- *Sales to customer cash receipts*
  + Decrease in accounts receivable
  − Increase in accounts receivable

Exhibit 16-3. Sample balance sheet.

	December 31 19X2	December 31 19X1	Increase (Decrease)
	ASSETS		
Current assets			
Cash	$ 12,500	$ 6,500	$ 6,000
Receivables, net	27,500	30,000	(2,500)
Inventories	47,000	40,000	7,000
Prepaid expenses	6,500	5,000	1,500
Total current assets	93,500	81,500	12,000
Fixed assets, net	171,500	132,500	39,000
Total assets	$265,000	$214,000	$51,000
	LIABILITIES AND SHAREHOLDERS' EQUITY		
Current liabilities			
Accounts payable	$ 16,000	$ 21,000	$ (5,000)
Income tax payable	1,000	500	500
Interest payable	500	1,500	(1,000)
Total current liabilities	17,500	23,000	(5,500)
Long-term debt			
Bonds payable	20,000	60,000	(40,000)
Shareholders' equity			
Common stock			
($2.00 par value)	175,000	100,000	75,000
Retained earnings	52,500	31,000	21,500
Total shareholders' equity	$227,500	$131,000	$96,500

- Cost of sales to cash payments to vendors from goods purchased
  + Increase in inventories
  − Decrease in inventories
  + Decrease in accounts payable
  − Increase in accounts payable
- Selling, general, and administrative expenses to cash payments for expenses
  + Increase in prepaid expenses
  − Decrease in prepaid expenses
  + Decrease in accrued liabilities
  − Increase in accrued liabilities

Exhibit 16-4. Statement of cash flows—indirect method with supplementary information.

The Corporation
Statement of Cash Flows
For the Year Ended December 31, 19X2

Net cash flows from operating activities		
Net income	$29,000	
Add (deduct) items to convert net income to cash basis		
Depreciation	6,500	
Accounts receivable decrease	2,500	
Inventory increase	(7,000)	
Prepaid expenses increase	(1,500)	
Accounts payable decrease	(5,000)	
Interest payable decrease	(1,000)	
Income tax payable increase	500	
Net cash provided by operating activities		$24,000
Cash flows from investing activities		
Sale of equipment	10,000	
Purchase of equipment	(30,000)	
Net cash used by investing activities		(20,000)
Cash flow from financing activities		
Issuance of common stock	50,000	
Retirement of bonds payable	(30,000)	
Payment of dividends	(5,000)	
Net cash provided by financing activities		15,000
Net increase in cash		19,000
Cash at beginning of year		6,500
Cash at end of year		$12,500
Supplemental cash flow information		
Cash paid for interest		$ 6,000
Cash paid for income taxes		$ 5,000
Issuance of common stock to acquire equipment		$15,000

- *Depreciation/amortization expenses*
  No impact on cash since these accounts are noncash in nature
- *Interest expense to cash payments to lenders for interest*
  + Decrease in interest payable
  − Increase in interest payable
- *Income tax expense to cash payments to governmental agencies for tax obligations*
  + Decrease in income tax payable
  − Increase in income tax payable

The result of these adjustments are reflected in the statement of cash flows shown in Exhibit 16-5 using the direct method. Exhibits 16-2 and 16-3 were used as the basis for preparation.

Benefits of Understanding the Statement of Cash Flows

The information provided in this chapter is important to investors, creditors, and other persons interested in assessing the financial condition of an organization. It is as important as the statement of income and the balance sheet in providing vital information about the company's current and future ability to grow and to provide adequate returns to its owners.

One major piece of information that is apparent from the statement of cash flows is whether an organization has the ability to generate cash flows in the future. A careful evaluation of the contents of the statement enables the user to compare, evaluate, and predict how much cash can be generated from operations and when. Over a period of time, this information acts as a barometer, enabling users to observe and analyze the financial ability of management to meet economic downturns, take advantage of expansion opportunities, promote sound investing and financing policies, and pay dividends to stockholders as well as interest and principal to creditors.

Since employees, creditors, and stockholders all require cash to meet their own obligations, they are particularly interested

Exhibit 16-5. Statement of cash flows—direct method with supplementary information.

The Corporation
Statement of Cash Flows
For the Year Ended December 31, 19X2

Cash flows from operating activities
Cash received from customers		$190,000
Cash paid to employees and suppliers	$155,000	
Cash paid for interest	6,000	
Cash paid for income taxes	5,000	166,000
Net cash provided by operating activities		24,000

Cash flows from investing activities
Sale of equipment	10,000	
Purchase of equipment	(30,000)	
Net cash used by investing activities		(20,000)

Cash flows from financing activities
Issuance of common stock	50,000	
Retirement of bonds payable	(30,000)	
Dividend payments	(5,000)	
Net cash provided by financing activities		15,000
Net increase in cash		19,000
Cash at beginning of year		6,500
Cash at end of year		$ 12,500

Reconciliation of net income to net cash flow from operating activities
Net income	$ 29,000
Add (deduct) items to convert net income to cash basis:	
Depreciation	6,500
Accounts receivable decrease	2,500
Inventory increase	(7,000)
Prepaid expenses increase	(1,500)
Accounts payable decrease	(5,000)
Interest payable decrease	(1,000)
Income tax payable increase	500
Net cash provided by operating activities	$ 24,000

Supplemental information
Issuance of common stock to acquire equipment	$ 15,000

in knowing how the company will meet its obligations to them—employees are concerned about salary and benefit increases; creditors about timely payments and corporate solvency in the future; and stockholders about the size of cash dividends, both now and in the future.

Stockholders and potential investors are interested in knowing how well a company manages its cash in operating activities, since the ability to manage cash and other resources in an effort to generate higher profits is crucial to the success of the organization. The statement of cash flows highlights this information.

How well a company invests its excess cash, allocates its resources, maintains its ability to borrow at reasonable rates, and finds opportunities in keeping with the organization's return strategy can be uncovered by reviewing the investing and financing activity sections of the statement. Knowing this information can help the reader better understand how the company operates and performs and therefore make better decisions.

It is important to note that the governing body of the accounting profession, the Financial and Accounting Standards Board (FASB), permits the use of both the direct and the indirect methods but prefers the direct. The indirect method is, however, more widely used.

Appendix A

Compound Interest Tables

Year	1%	2%	3%	4%	5%	6%	7%	8%	9%	10%
1	1.010	1.020	1.030	1.040	1.050	1.060	1.070	1.080	1.090	1.100
2	1.020	1.040	1.061	1.082	1.102	1.124	1.145	1.166	1.188	1.210
3	1.030	1.061	1.093	1.125	1.156	1.191	1.225	1.260	1.295	1.331
4	1.041	1.082	1.126	1.170	1.216	1.262	1.311	1.360	1.412	1.464
5	1.051	1.104	1.159	1.217	1.276	1.338	1.403	1.469	1.539	1.611
6	1.062	1.120	1.194	1.265	1.340	1.419	1.501	1.587	1.677	1.772
7	1.072	1.149	1.230	1.316	1.407	1.504	1.606	1.714	1.828	1.949
8	1.083	1.172	1.267	1.369	1.477	1.594	1.718	1.851	1.993	2.144
9	1.094	1.195	1.305	1.423	1.551	1.689	1.838	1.999	2.172	2.358
10	1.105	1.219	1.344	1.480	1.629	1.791	1.967	2.159	2.367	2.594
11	1.116	1.243	1.384	1.539	1.710	1.898	2.105	2.332	2.580	2.853
12	1.127	1.268	1.426	1.601	1.796	2.012	2.252	2.518	2.813	3.138
13	1.138	1.294	1.469	1.665	1.886	2.133	2.410	2.720	3.066	3.452
14	1.149	1.319	1.513	1.732	1.980	2.261	2.579	2.937	3.342	3.797
15	1.161	1.346	1.558	1.801	2.079	2.397	2.759	3.172	3.642	4.177
16	1.173	1.373	1.605	1.873	2.183	2.540	2.952	3.426	3.970	4.595
17	1.184	1.400	1.653	1.948	2.292	2.693	3.159	3.700	4.328	5.054
18	1.196	1.428	1.702	2.026	2.407	2.854	3.380	3.996	4.717	5.560
19	1.208	1.457	1.754	2.107	2.527	3.026	3.617	4.316	5.142	6.116
20	1.220	1.486	1.806	2.191	2.653	3.207	3.870	4.661	5.604	6.728
25	1.282	1.641	2.094	2.666	3.386	4.292	5.427	6.848	8.632	10.835
30	1.348	1.811	2.427	3.243	4.322	5.743	7.612	10.063	13.268	17.449

Year	12%	14%	16%	18%	20%	24%	28%	32%	40%	50%
1	1.120	1.140	1.160	1.180	1.200	1.240	1.280	1.320	1.400	1.500
2	1.254	1.300	1.346	1.392	1.440	1.538	1.638	1.742	1.960	2.250
3	1.405	1.482	1.561	1.643	1.728	1.907	2.067	2.300	2.744	3.375
4	1.574	1.689	1.811	1.939	2.074	2.364	2.684	3.036	3.842	5.062
5	1.762	1.925	2.100	2.288	2.488	2.932	3.436	4.007	5.378	7.594
6	1.974	2.195	2.436	2.700	2.986	3.635	4.398	5.290	7.530	11.391
7	2.211	2.502	2.826	3.185	3.583	4.508	5.629	6.983	10.541	17.086
8	2.476	2.853	3.278	3.759	4.300	5.590	7.206	9.217	14.758	25.629
9	2.773	3.252	3.803	4.435	5.160	6.931	9.223	12.166	20.661	38.443
10	3.106	3.707	4.411	5.234	6.192	8.594	11.806	16.060	28.925	57.665
11	3.479	4.226	5.117	6.176	7.430	10.657	15.112	21.199	40.496	86.498
12	3.896	4.818	5.936	7.288	8.916	13.215	19.343	27.983	56.694	129.746
13	4.363	5.492	6.886	8.599	10.699	16.386	24.759	36.937	79.372	194.619
14	4.887	6.261	7.988	10.147	12.839	20.319	31.691	48.757	111.120	291.929
15	5.474	7.138	9.266	11.074	15.407	25.196	40.565	64.350	155.568	437.894
16	6.130	8.137	10.748	14.129	18.488	31.243	51.923	84.954	217.795	656.840
17	6.866	9.276	12.468	16.672	22.186	38.741	66.461	112.140	304.914	985.260
18	7.690	10.575	14.463	19.673	26.623	48.039	85.071	148.020	426.879	1477.900
19	8.613	12.056	16.777	23.214	31.948	59.568	108.890	195.390	597.630	2216.800
20	9.646	13.743	19.461	27.393	38.338	73.864	139.380	257.920	836.683	3325.300
25	17.000	26.462	40.874	62.669	95.396	216.542	478.900	1033.600	4499.880	25251.000
30	29.960	50.950	85.850	143.371	237.376	634.820	1645.500	4142.100	24201.432	191750.000

Appendix B

Present
Value Tables

Year	1%	2%	3%	4%	5%	6%	7%	8%	9%	10%
1	0.9901	0.9804	0.9709	0.9615	0.9524	0.9434	0.9346	0.9259	0.9174	0.9091
2	0.9803	0.9612	0.9426	0.9246	0.9070	0.8900	0.8734	0.8573	0.8417	0.8264
3	0.9706	0.9423	0.9151	0.8890	0.8638	0.8396	0.8163	0.7938	0.7722	0.7513
4	0.9610	0.9238	0.8885	0.8548	0.8227	0.7921	0.7629	0.7350	0.7084	0.6830
5	0.9515	0.9057	0.8626	0.8219	0.7835	0.7473	0.7130	0.6806	0.6499	0.6209
6	0.9420	0.8880	0.8375	0.7903	0.7462	0.7050	0.6663	0.6302	0.5963	0.5645
7	0.9327	0.8706	0.8131	0.7599	0.7107	0.6651	0.6227	0.5835	0.5470	0.5132
8	0.9235	0.8535	0.7894	0.7307	0.6768	0.6274	0.5820	0.5403	0.5019	0.4665
9	0.9143	0.8368	0.7664	0.7026	0.6446	0.5919	0.5439	0.5002	0.4604	0.4241
10	0.9053	0.8203	0.7441	0.6756	0.6139	0.5584	0.5083	0.4632	0.4224	0.3855
11	0.8963	0.8043	0.7224	0.6496	0.5847	0.5268	0.4751	0.4289	0.3875	0.3505
12	0.8874	0.7885	0.7014	0.6246	0.5568	0.4970	0.4440	0.3971	0.3555	0.3186
13	0.8787	0.7730	0.6810	0.6006	0.5303	0.4688	0.4150	0.3677	0.3262	0.2987
14	0.8700	0.7579	0.6611	0.5775	0.5051	0.4423	0.3878	0.3405	0.2992	0.2633
15	0.8613	0.7430	0.6419	0.5553	0.4810	0.4173	0.3624	0.3152	0.2745	0.2394

16	0.8528	0.7284	0.6232	0.5339	0.4581	0.3936	0.3387	0.2919	0.2519	0.2176
17	0.8444	0.7142	0.6050	0.5134	0.4363	0.3714	0.3166	0.2703	0.2311	0.1978
18	0.8360	0.7002	0.5874	0.4936	0.4155	0.3503	0.2959	0.2502	0.2120	0.1799
19	0.8277	0.6864	0.5703	0.4746	0.3957	0.3305	0.2765	0.2317	0.1945	0.1635
20	0.8195	0.6730	0.5537	0.4564	0.3769	0.3118	0.2584	0.2145	0.1784	0.1486
21	0.8114	0.6598	0.5375	0.4388	0.3589	0.2942	0.2415	0.1987	0.1637	0.1351
22	0.8034	0.6468	0.5219	0.4220	0.3418	0.2775	0.2257	0.1839	0.1502	0.1228
23	0.7954	0.6342	0.5067	0.4057	0.3256	0.2618	0.2109	0.1703	0.1378	0.1117
24	0.7876	0.6217	0.4919	0.3901	0.3101	0.2470	0.1971	0.1577	0.1264	0.1015
25	0.7798	0.6095	0.4776	0.3751	0.2953	0.2330	0.1842	0.1460	0.1160	0.0923
26	0.7720	0.5976	0.4637	0.3607	0.2812	0.2198	0.1722	0.1352	0.1064	0.0839
27	0.7644	0.5859	0.4502	0.3468	0.2678	0.2074	0.1609	0.1252	0.0976	0.0763
38	0.7568	0.5744	0.4371	0.3335	0.2552	0.1956	0.1504	0.1159	0.0895	0.0693
29	0.7493	0.5631	0.4243	0.3207	0.2429	0.1846	0.1406	0.1073	0.0822	0.0630
30	0.7419	0.5521	0.4120	0.3083	0.2314	0.1741	0.1314	0.0994	0.0754	0.0573

Year	11%	12%	13%	14%	15%	16%	17%	18%	19%	20%
1	0.9009	0.8929	0.8850	0.8772	0.8696	0.8621	0.8547	0.8475	0.8403	0.8333
2	0.8116	0.7972	0.7831	0.7695	0.7561	0.7432	0.7305	0.7182	0.7062	0.6944
3	0.7312	0.7118	0.6913	0.6750	0.6575	0.6407	0.6244	0.6086	0.5934	0.5787
4	0.6587	0.6355	0.6133	0.5921	0.5718	0.5523	0.5337	0.5158	0.4987	0.4823
5	0.5935	0.5674	0.5428	0.5194	0.4972	0.4761	0.4561	0.4371	0.4190	0.4019
6	0.5346	0.5066	0.4803	0.4556	0.4323	0.4104	0.3898	0.3704	0.3521	0.3349
7	0.4817	0.4523	0.4251	0.3996	0.3759	0.3538	0.3332	0.3139	0.2959	0.2791
8	0.4339	0.4039	0.3762	0.3506	0.3269	0.3050	0.2848	0.2660	0.2487	0.2326
9	0.3909	0.3606	0.3329	0.3075	0.2843	0.2630	0.2434	0.2255	0.2090	0.1938
10	0.3522	0.3220	0.2946	0.2697	0.2472	0.2267	0.2080	0.1911	0.1756	0.1615
11	0.3173	0.2875	0.2607	0.2366	0.2149	0.1954	0.1778	0.1619	0.1476	0.1346
12	0.2858	0.2567	0.2307	0.2076	0.1869	0.1685	0.1520	0.1372	0.1240	0.1122
13	0.2575	0.2292	0.2042	0.1821	0.1625	0.1452	0.1299	0.1163	0.1042	0.0935
14	0.2320	0.2046	0.1807	0.1597	0.1413	0.1252	0.1110	0.0985	0.0876	0.0779
15	0.2090	0.1827	0.1599	0.1401	0.1229	0.1079	0.0949	0.0835	0.0736	0.0649

16	0.1883	0.1631	0.1415	0.1229	0.1069	0.0930	0.0811	0.0708	0.0618	0.0541
17	0.1696	0.1456	0.1252	0.1078	0.0929	0.0802	0.0693	0.0600	0.0520	0.0451
18	0.1528	0.1300	0.1108	0.0946	0.0808	0.0691	0.0592	0.0508	0.0437	0.0376
19	0.1377	0.1161	0.0981	0.0829	0.0703	0.0596	0.0506	0.0431	0.0367	0.0313
20	0.1240	0.1037	0.0868	0.0728	0.0611	0.0514	0.0433	0.0365	0.0308	0.0261
21	0.1117	0.0926	0.0768	0.0638	0.0531	0.0443	0.0370	0.0309	0.0259	0.0217
22	0.1007	0.0826	0.0680	0.0560	0.0462	0.0382	0.0316	0.0262	0.0218	0.0181
23	0.0907	0.0738	0.0601	0.0491	0.0402	0.0329	0.0270	0.0222	0.0183	0.0151
24	0.0817	0.0659	0.0532	0.0431	0.0349	0.0284	0.0231	0.0188	0.0154	0.0126
25	0.0736	0.0588	0.0471	0.0378	0.0304	0.0245	0.0197	0.0160	0.0129	0.0105
26	0.0663	0.0525	0.0417	0.0331	0.0264	0.0211	0.0169	0.0135	0.0109	0.0087
27	0.0597	0.0469	0.0369	0.0291	0.0230	0.0182	0.0144	0.0115	0.0091	0.0073
28	0.0538	0.0419	0.0326	0.0255	0.0200	0.0157	0.0123	0.0097	0.0077	0.0061
29	0.0485	0.0374	0.0289	0.0224	0.0174	0.0135	0.0105	0.0082	0.0064	0.0051
30	0.0437	0.0334	0.0256	0.0196	0.0151	0.0116	0.0090	0.0070	0.0054	0.0042

Year	21%	22%	23%	24%	25%	26%	27%	28%	29%	30%
1	0.8264	0.8197	0.8130	0.8065	0.8000	0.7937	0.7874	0.7813	0.7752	0.7692
2	0.6830	0.6719	0.6610	0.6504	0.6400	0.6299	0.6200	0.6104	0.6009	0.5917
3	0.5645	0.5507	0.5374	0.5245	0.5120	0.4999	0.4882	0.4768	0.4658	0.4552
4	0.4665	0.4514	0.4369	0.4230	0.4096	0.3968	0.3844	0.3725	0.3611	0.3501
5	0.3855	0.3700	0.3552	0.3411	0.3277	0.3149	0.3027	0.2910	0.2799	0.2693
6	0.3186	0.3033	0.2888	0.2751	0.2621	0.2499	0.2383	0.2274	0.2170	0.2072
7	0.2633	0.2486	0.2348	0.2218	0.2097	0.1983	0.1877	0.1776	0.1682	0.1594
8	0.2176	0.2038	0.1909	0.1789	0.1678	0.1574	0.1478	0.1388	0.1304	0.1226
9	0.1799	0.1670	0.1552	0.1443	0.1342	0.1249	0.1164	0.1084	0.1011	0.0943
10	0.1486	0.1369	0.1262	0.1164	0.1074	0.0992	0.0916	0.0847	0.0784	0.0725
11	0.1228	0.1122	0.1026	0.0938	0.0859	0.0787	0.0721	0.0662	0.0607	0.0558
12	0.1015	0.0920	0.0834	0.0757	0.0687	0.0625	0.0568	0.0517	0.0471	0.0429
13	0.0839	0.0754	0.0678	0.0610	0.0550	0.0496	0.0447	0.0404	0.0365	0.0330
14	0.0693	0.0618	0.0551	0.0492	0.0440	0.0393	0.0352	0.0316	0.0283	0.0253
15	0.0573	0.0507	0.0448	0.0397	0.0352	0.0312	0.0277	0.0247	0.0219	0.0195

16	0.0474	0.0415	0.0364	0.0320	0.0281	0.0248	0.0218	0.0193	0.0170	0.0150
17	0.0391	0.0340	0.0296	0.0258	0.0225	0.0197	0.0172	0.0150	0.0132	0.0116
18	0.0323	0.0279	0.0241	0.0208	0.0180	0.0156	0.0135	0.0118	0.0102	0.0089
19	0.0267	0.0229	0.0196	0.0168	0.0144	0.0124	0.0107	0.0092	0.0079	0.0068
20	0.0221	0.0187	0.0159	0.0135	0.0115	0.0098	0.0084	0.0072	0.0061	0.0053
21	0.0183	0.0154	0.0129	0.0109	0.0092	0.0078	0.0066	0.0056	0.0048	0.0040
22	0.0151	0.0126	0.0105	0.0088	0.0074	0.0062	0.0052	0.0044	0.0037	0.0031
23	0.0125	0.0103	0.0086	0.0071	0.0059	0.0049	0.0041	0.0034	0.0029	0.0024
24	0.0103	0.0085	0.0070	0.0057	0.0047	0.0039	0.0032	0.0027	0.0022	0.0018
25	0.0085	0.0069	0.0057	0.0046	0.0038	0.0031	0.0025	0.0021	0.0017	0.0014
26	0.0070	0.0057	0.0046	0.0037	0.0030	0.0025	0.0020	0.0016	0.0013	0.0011
27	0.0058	0.0047	0.0037	0.0030	0.0024	0.0019	0.0016	0.0013	0.0010	0.0008
28	0.0048	0.0038	0.0030	0.0024	0.0019	0.0015	0.0012	0.0010	0.0008	0.0006
29	0.0040	0.0031	0.0025	0.0020	0.0015	0.0012	0.0010	0.0008	0.0006	0.0005
30	0.0033	0.0026	0.0020	0.0016	0.0012	0.0010	0.0008	0.0006	0.0005	0.0004

Years	35%	40%	45%	50%
1	0.741	0.714	0.690	0.667
2	0.549	0.510	0.476	0.444
3	0.406	0.364	0.328	0.296
4	0.301	0.260	0.226	0.198
5	0.223	0.186	0.156	0.132
6	0.165	0.133	0.108	0.088
7	0.122	0.095	0.074	0.059
8	0.091	0.068	0.051	0.039
9	0.067	0.048	0.035	0.026
10	0.050	0.035	0.024	0.017
11	0.037	0.025	0.017	0.012
12	0.027	0.018	0.012	0.008
13	0.020	0.013	0.008	0.005
14	0.015	0.009	0.006	0.003
15	0.011	0.006	0.004	0.002
16	0.008	0.005	0.003	0.002
17	0.006	0.003	0.002	0.001
18	0.005	0.002	0.001	0.001
19	0.003	0.002	0.001	
20	0.002	0.001	0.001	
21	0.002	0.001		
22	0.001	0.001		
23	0.001			
24	0.001			
25	0.001			
26				
27				
38				
29				
30				

Index

Breinigsville, PA USA
18 January 2011
253590BV00004B/23/P